Innis/McLuh

New World Perspectives

HAROLD INNIS/MARSHALL McLUHAN/GEORGE GRANT
Arthur Kroker

Forthcoming
C. WRIGHT MILLS/PAUL BARAN/ROBERT LINDER
Russell Jacoby

C. B. MACPHERSON
William Leiss

MARGARET LAURENCE/MARGARET ATWOOD
Eileen Manion

FERNAND DUMONT
Michael A. Weinstein

MARSHALL McLUHAN
John Fekete

MARCEL RIOUX
Raymond Morrow/Greg Nielsen

MICHAEL ONDAATJE
Eli Mandel

HUBERT AQUIN
Michael Dorland

NORTHROP FRYE
David Cook

THORSTEIN VEBLEN
Andrew Wernick

also

MARY O'BRIEN
ADRIENNE RICH
JOHN PORTER
RENÉ LÉVESQUE/PIERRE E. TRUDEAU
TALCOTT PARSONS
GEORGE WOODCOCK
SUSAN SONTAG
J. K. GALBRAITH
CHARLES TAYLOR
OCTAVIO PAZ
FREDRIC JAMESON
and others

TECHNOLOGY AND THE CANADIAN MIND

Innis/McLuhan/Grant

Arthur Kroker

New World Perspectives

Montréal 1984

                New World Perspectives/Perspectives Nouveau Monde
                3930 Parc Lafontaine
                Montréal, Québec
                H2L 3M6

Canadian Cataloguing in Publication Data

Kroker, Arthur, 1945 –
    Technology and the Canadian Mind: Innis/McLuhan/Grant

(New World perspectives)
Bibliography; p.
ISBN 0-920393-00-4

1. Technology — Social aspects — Canada.
2. Technology and civilization.
3. Grant, George, 1918 -   .
4. Innis, Harold, 1894 - 1952.
5. McLuhan, Marshall, 1911 - 1980.

I. Title.   II. Series

CB478.K76 1984   303.4'83'0971   C84-090112-7

Printed and bound in Canada

CONTENTS

For their helpful comments and close readings of the
manuscript, I am grateful to Marilouise Kroker,
Daniel Drache, Michael Dorland, David Cook
and Michael Weinstein. I would also like to
thank Alexis Gosselin.

1

The Canadian Discourse

Canada's principal contribution to North American thought consists of a highly original, comprehensive, and eloquent discourse on technology.

What makes the discourse on technology such a central aspect of the Canadian imagination is that this discourse is situated *midway* between the future of the New World and the past of European culture, between the rapid unfolding of the "technological imperative" in American empire and the classical origins of the technological dynamo in European history. The Canadian discourse is neither the American way nor the European way, but an oppositional culture trapped midway between economy and history. This is to say that the Canadian mind is that of the *in-between*: a restless oscillation between the pragmatic will to live at all costs of the Americans and a searing lament for that which has been suppressed by the modern, technical order. The essence of the Canadian intellectual condition is this: it is our fate by virtue of historical circumstance and geographical accident to be forever marginal to the "present-mindedness" of American culture (a society which specializing as it does in the public ethic of "instrumental activism" does not enjoy the recriminations of historical remembrance); and to be incapable of being more than ambivalent on the cultural legacy of our European past. At work in the Canadian mind is, in fact, a great and dynamic polarity between technology and culture, between economy and landscape. And this dialectical movement between the power of American empire and our bitter historical knowledge that the crisis has its origins much deeper in European culture is the gamble of the Canadian discourse on technology. The Canadian mind may be one of the main sites in modern times for working-out the meaning of technological experience.

Indeed, a general fascination with the question of technology extends like a brilliant arc across the Canadian cultural imagination, from cinema and music to literature and philosophy.

In rock music, the Canadian group, Rush, has been embraced by a wider North American audience because in songs like *New World Man* ("He's a rebel and a runner; a stop-light turning green"), it has captured the dynamic *willing* which is at the centre of technological society. On the opposite side of the musical imagination, there is the tragic lament of Bruce Cockburn who, in songs such as *The Trouble With Normal* and *Civilization and its Discontents*, provides a haunting reminder of that which has been lost by our absorption into the fully modern technical empire of the United States. In Canadian art, the fateful meeting of technology and land was the great tension first, and most brilliantly, explored by the Group of Seven in the 1930s, and which now forms the basic thematic of so much of Canadian painting, from the *realism* of Pratt and Colville in the Maritimes to the *technological surrealism* of Ivan Eyre in the prairies. In literature, Northrop Frye's remark in *The Educated Imagination* that we live now in a "gigantic techno-logical skyscraper" finds its echo in Margaret Atwood's searing reflections on the "anxiety structures" at the heart of techno-logical society. And, of course, there can be few more tortured accounts of the nihilism which spreads out through the technological experience than Dennis Lee's *Savage Fields* or, for that matter, Alice Munro's description of the dread and deep anxiety which is everywhere now in modern society. In cinema, Don Shebib's *Goin' Down the Road* is a powerful and evocative description of the fundamental human tragedy (in this film, the forced depopulation of the Atlantic provinces with its all too familiar internal exile of Maritimers to the "centre society" of Toronto) which accompanies radical changes in the technical base of Canada's political economy. But if *Goin' Down the Road* provides a haunting feature-length account of the relationship of technology and dependency, then it must also be said that the celebrated and pioneering animation productions of the National Film Board of Canada as well disclose the meeting of the creative imagination and technology in the Canadian mind.

Finally, there exists in every major city, from Montréal and Halifax to Toronto, Calgary and Vancouver aggressive displays of the architecture of hi-tech: building designs which say everything about the intractation of technology in the Canadian identity, and symbolize how deeply and intensely the Canadian fate is entangled with the dynamic momentum of the techno-logical experience in North America. In Toronto, that privi-leged outpost of American empire, there are to be found two brilliant and unforgettable displays of hi-tech building design, both of which reveal how central *technique* is to Canadian identity. The first of these is the famous CN Tower: an almost perfect phallocentric symbol of the union of power and technology in the making of the Canadian discourse. The CN Tower is a powerful reminder of our immersion in the processed world of communication technologies: it combines function (communication), entertainment (restaurants and tours), and corporate ideology (the tower is a *sign* of Toronto's entry into the modern project). And this display of techno-cratic architecture is also a vivid reminder of the degree to which Canadian experience has been shaped by the spread of communication technologies (the railway, radio, television, telegraph, and microwave transmissions) across the landscape; for hi-tech communications has drawn us deeply into the cultural discourse of American empire. The CN Tower is only a *visible sign* of what is happening to us, invisibly and impercep-

Toronto's CN Tower

tibly, as we are processed through the new information order of technological society. Indeed, the bold, almost primitive, architecture of the CN Tower may reveal a basic truth about Canadian political existence as a perfect ideological symbol of the "technological nationalism" which has always been the essence of the Canadian state, and, most certainly, the locus of the Canadian identity.[1] Ironically, as if to demonstrate that the production of Canada in the image of technology has made of us suitable candidates for full admission to a creative leadership role in the technological dynamo of the United States, there is just to the side of the CN Tower another, almost grisly, display of technocratic architecture: the equally famous Royal Bank Plaza. What is most unusual about the Royal Bank Plaza is not its sheer size or even its almost totalitarian design. In the best of hi-tech corporate design, the towers are all glass and steel: the windows are impervious to the human gaze and the building is designed to screen off nature (and ourselves) by its mirror-like reflection of the external environment. As measures of corporate swagger, there are bigger and even more demonic buildings in Chicago, New York, Los Angeles, or Tokyo. But the Royal Bank Plaza presents itself as a particularly Canadian mediation of society, and a closed, circular one at that. In a sharp reminder of the Narcissus theme*, the Plaza reflects that we are in the presence of a closed semiological system which provides its own identity in a never-ending circular loop of information load and feed-back. If the Royal Bank Plaza is also a visible symbol of how we are worked and reworked within the medium of modern technology, then this is a lesson which is taught everyday in the designed environments of the banks and life-insurance companies which dominate the visual landscape of Canadian cities.

What distinguishes the Royal Bank Plaza from all other such massive and, indeed, overwhelming examples of technocratic design, and what makes of its architecture such a radical break from the received Canadian preference for a "civilized", but deferential, culture is that this corporate edifice is coloured a brilliant, gleaming *gold* — as ostentatious and dynamic a symbol as could be created for Canada's claim, at least in the world of high finance, to a leading position in the bourgeois world of technology and empire. In this "new order" bank-building, money fuses with technique into an entirely new aesthetic. An announcement is made in the silent language of architecture: Canada is in the American age now, an era in which the restless expansion of the technological empire of the United States is coeval with the reduction of every vestige of Canadian experience to the will to money or, what is the same, to the driving will to power. To the extent that Canadian literature, film, and music often disclose, in a discourse which is nuanced and poignant, the full ambivalence of life in the technological sensorium; to the same extent, the mass media of television and architecture reveal that the technological experience also has its seductive side — the absorbing, carnivalesque and often hysterical world of

---

* So dear to a technological thinker like McLuhan or a technological filmmaker like Norman McLaren.

consumer culture. But whether viewed from the side of domination or seduction, the lesson is the same: the Canadian identity is, and always has been, fully integral to the question of technology. Indeed, a sustained and intensive reflection on the meaning of the technological experience *is* the Canadian discourse.

What is at stake in the Canadian discourse on technology is always the same: the urgent sense that the full significance of technological society (typified by the haunting images of the "information society", the politics of the "technological imperative", computerland and pay-TV) cannot be understood within its own, narrow terms of reference. For Canadian thinkers, technological society jeopardizes at a fundamental level the received traditions of western culture, and makes of our fate as North Americans a journey, almost a skywalk, into an unknown future. As Atwood said: there's "menace" everywhere now; and as others, from Dennis Lee to George Grant and Marshall McLuhan have replied: it is also our "identity" which is wagered in the coming-to-be of the society of technique.

The Canadian discourse is, then, a way of seeking to recover a voice by which to articulate a different historical possibility against the present closure of the technological order. The Québec sociologist, Marcel Rioux, once said that "to be a Québécois is to agree to live dangerously";[2] in the same way, to enter into the Canadian discourse on technology is also to participate in a dangerous venture where everything is at stake and where nothing is guaranteed. In reflecting on the relationship of technology and culture, and this in the double sense of the relationship between technology and civilization *and* between technology and power, Canadian thought forces the question of what is the most appropriate response to the technological dynamo. American thought has always privileged the relationship of technology and society; in Canada, it is "self", not society, that is privileged. That is why so much of Canadian thought is at the forefront of the modern mind in thinking through the deepest meanings of technological society. It is also why the Canadian discourse is so existential: from the "tragic self" of George Grant, to the "victim positions" of Margaret Atwood, to McLuhan's "cosmic man", and, finally, to Dennis Lee's despairing self trapped between an irrecoverable past and a hopeless future.[3]

Innis/McLuhan/Grant

The Canadian discourse on technology is then a privileged one. It is fully implicated in the "spearhead of modernity" of the United States. This is a national tradition of thought which has been steeled by the fantastic pressures of technology and empire which threaten to exterminate any indigenous, popular culture, in Québec or English-Canada. But the Canadian discourse also represents a courageous, and creative, struggle to think outside of and against the closed horizons of technological society. The Canadian mind seeks to *preserve*, if only in memory, those valuable aspects of experience which have been obliterated by the technological experience; or, alternatively, to *emancipate* technology from within by rethinking the meaning of science and technology.

Thus for every thinker like Marshall McLuhan who had a fully cosmopolitan mind, and in the pure media of electromagnetic technology the first of the genuinely "electronic minds" (an Aquinas of the electronic age); for every politician like David Crombie, who at a recent Conservative convention, perhaps carried away by the hysteria of the moment and by the chance to corral the Red Tory vote with a technocratic come-on, said of the Canadian identity that we were the "new voyageurs of the electronic age"; and for every writer like Margaret Atwood who reveals an important dimension of the technocratic imagination when she says "I am a site where action happens", there is another, opposing side of the Canadian mind.

This is the side of a sometimes poetic, always tragic, reflection on the price to be paid for the consumer comforts of technological society. This is the side of George Grant's scathing critique of the "capitalist suburbia of social engineers"; of Dallas Smythe's exploration of the political economy of Canadian communications as *Dependency Road*; of the McLean Brothers' musical tribute to Canadian life, *Bitter Reality*; and of Patricia Marchak's pioneering studies of the deep relationship between technology and dependency in

Canadian economic history.[4] Indeed, if it is appropriate to describe the trajectory of thought traced by McLuhan, Frye, Atwood and Trudeau ("technology as reason") as *technological humanism*,[5] then it might also be said that on the far side of the Canadian mind, on its dark side, there exists the opposing perspective of *technological dependency*. Technological humanism seeks to renew technique from within by releasing the creative possibilities inherent in the technological experience. Thus McLuhan writes of the contemporary century as an age of a potentially new "Finn cycle"; a "cosmic" era in which the exercise of "mythic, integral, and in-depth participation" in the electronic media, from computers to television, will create the conditions for a new *pentecostal* condition. Technology as the Tower of Babel, but this time in the New Wave terms of the electronic media. And technological humanism can be so expansive, pluralistic, universalistic, and creative (sort of a "mini-United Nations") because it privileges the relationship of technology and freedom. But the perspective of technological dependency is just the opposite. This is an angle of vision on the technological experience which focusses on technology as the locus of human domination: sometimes in terms of a "dependent" political economy (Drache, Watkins, Marchak, Smythe, Clement);[6] sometimes in literary terms as the loss of cultural heritage (Margaret Laurence, Alice Munro, Eli Mandel);[7] but more often in deep philosophical terms as the unleashing in North America of almost demonic forces deep in the western mind. Thus while McLuhan may urge that we "blast" through to the new electronic age, George Grant reminds us that our fate as North Americans is to live as dying "gasping political fish", suffering an oxygen-starvation of morality and vision in the midst of the technological dynamo. Grant is the Nietzsche of the New World to this extent: he says that "technique is ourselves" and that, consequently, our permanent condition as technical beings is to endure "intimations of deprival": the loss even of a *sense* of loss of the human good which has been expunged by technological society. McLuhan may rush south to the United States; Grant is different. He is a self-professed Haligonian philosopher ("Halifax is the spiritual centre of Canada") who has perfectly caught the violent, and often demonic, spirit of twentieth-century experience. Grant gives us dependency theory in new key: an eloquent meditation on the complexity of our entanglement in the technological experience. In a word, Grant has done the impossible. From within the horizon of the technological dynamo, he has "enucleated" the meaning of modern life as the mastery of technique. And he has done so in a way that expands the meaning of technological experience beyond technique to include the modes of organization (technocratic bureaucracies), ideology (liberalism), and public morality (instrumental activism) associated with the development of technology in North America.

George Grant and Marshall McLuhan are emblematic figures in Canadian thought. Their competing perspectives on technology represent at once the limits and the possibilities of the Canadian mind. Indeed, Grant and McLuhan stand to one another as bi-polar opposites on the question of technology, because each thinker provides the most intensive and elaborate account possible of two classic angles of vision which Canadian thought has contributed to the study of technology. McLuhan is the leading exemplar of the perspective of technological humanism; and Grant is the most important representative in Canadian thought of the perspective of technological dependency. But if McLuhan and Grant are the polar opposites of the Canadian mind, this can only mean that there must be a *third perspective* in the Canadian discourse on technology which mediates technological humanism and technological dependency. And this is the critical perspective of *technological realism*, whose leading advocate is the political economist, Harold A. Innis. Grant may write a tragic "lament" and McLuhan might privilege the "utopian" possibilities of technology, but Innis' ideal was always of attaining "balance and proportion" between the competing claims of empire (power) and culture (history). To Grant's concentration on the recovery of a sense of "time" against the spatializing qualities of the electronic media (*Time as History*) and to McLuhan's almost giddy celebration of "space" as the locus of modern experience (*The Medium is the Massage*), Innis appealed in *Empire and Communications* as well as in *The Bias of Communication* for a reintegration of "time and space" in western experience. Thus while Grant is a tragic philosopher to

McLuhan's happy rhetorician, Innis always remained a political economist of the blood.

From the *Fur Trade in Canada* to *The Cod Fisheries* to his last works on technology and civilization, Innis never lost sight of the fully ambivalent fate of Canada in the New World. In his estimation, technology always contained paradoxical tendencies to freedom and domination simultaneously. The Canadian Pacific Railway may have extended "European civilization" in technical form across the Canadian prairies; it also gave rise to an entirely new political dynamic, one which pitted emergent, populist forces in the Canadian West against the "acquisitive and selfish" economic instincts of the Ontario bourgeoisie. In Innis' perspective, the truth of technological experience was never to be discovered in the extremes of dependency or humanism, but in their recombination into a dynamic, new third term. Consequently, Innis was the thinker who, refusing to restrict his inquiry to the "centre" or the "margin" or, what is the same, to privilege either "centrifugal or centripetal tendencies" in Canadian experience, always insisted on keeping the tension alive between the opposing tendencies to domination and emancipation in technological society. Innis was a technological realist in this sense: he wished to create an enduring and dynamic synthesis in the Canadian mind between the warring impulses of technology and civilization. That Innis was a critical historian to McLuhan's the formalist and an expansive economist and culture critic to Grant's the philosophical despond, only meant that he was the last and best of all the Canadian thinkers. For better or for worse, the Canadian imagination privileges historical discourse as much as it shows an almost instinctual attraction for the realist mediation over the more spectacular, but limited, appeals of utopia or dependency. That Innis went to his death knowing the *immobilisme* at the heart of his intellectual project only indicated a thinker who, running alongside and in accordance with deep Canadian prejudices towards the historical and the realist compromise, was almost paradigmatic of the impossibility of Canadian culture. In his classic essay, "The Political Implications of Unused Capacity", Innis could say that "frontier countries are storm centres to the international economy" because he knew that if it was the Canadian fate to be Athens (civilization) to the American Rome (power), then, and this so bitterly, was one case where the imperial empire refused to reciprocate the civilizing moment. Canada was a "civilizing culture" with no place to go.

Thus the eloquent and forceful perspectives of George Grant, Marshall McLuhan and Harold Innis structure the Canadian discourse on technology. Taken separately, each of their perspectives provides important insights into specific dimensions of the technological experience. In a way even more striking than Jacques Ellul's *The Technological Society*, George Grant elicits an austere and fundamental account of the unravelling of technique as the dynamic locus of the modern century. Grant explores the psychological and political detritus of a society which has linked its fate to the "language of willing." Grant's writing moves at that edge where political history passes over instantaneously into political biography. Using language as a "probe" to blast through the deep, invisible assumptions of the technological media within which we are situated, McLuhan provides a galaxy of insights into the meaning of the "technical extensions" of human experience. Aphorism, jest, bombast, ironic counterpoint: these are only some of the literary devices used by McLuhan to paint the technological experience in the most *dramatic* of baroque terms. Over and beyond the liberal imagination of Daniel Bell and Lewis Mumford, McLuhan's perspective on the electronic age could achieve such global acclaim just because he succeeded, where others had failed, in deciphering the inner, structural code of the technological experience. And McLuhan could be such a brilliant encrypter of the technological media because he was, first and foremost, an artist who understood the desperate need to learn a new "perspective", an alternative way of looking, at the processed world of technology. And what of Innis, this fully ambivalent and, as yet, unassimilated thinker (whose intellectual legacy is represented by an exhaustive and highly original series of pioneering studies of Canadian economic history *and* by formative studies of the "bias of communication" in western culture)? Innis' perspective on technology is the wound in Canadian thought which refuses to close. Outside the grim existentialism of George Grant and beyond the Catholic humanism of Marshall McLuhan, Innis' contribution, while less spectacular, was perhaps more permanent. For Innis provides us with an entirely original *methodological* approach to the study of technology: with a way of examining the interplay of technique, commerce, culture, and social relations as textured and layered in its interpretative strategy as it is critical and democratic in its intellectual impulses. Innis made the study of technology and civilization (Canada as a big "staples commodity") an opportunity for the development of a distinctively Canadian way of thinking. In the Innisian world of technological realism, there emerges an epistemological toolkit for the exploration of dependency and emancipation as the two faces of technological society. Innis' thought is perfectly styled to the historical specificity of Canada's political economy and culture because it is a constant reflection on the great tension between centre/periphery in Canada's historical formation.

But if, *considered separately*, the brilliant perspectives of Innis, McLuhan and Grant provide privileged accounts of different dimensions of the technological experience, then, *taken together*, these viewpoints represent the major positions which might be adopted today on the question of technology. The discourse on technology, as expressed by the clash of perspectives among Grant, McLuhan and Innis, has an intellectual, and political, significance which extends well beyond the Canadian circumstance. Indeed, it may well be that, with the spread of the consumer culture of the United States (driven on by the *forced* technological imperative of the electronic media) around the *processed* globe, the perspectives of technological humanism, technological dependency, and technological realism may represent the limits of the human response to the lead-forces of modern society. If this is so, then it must also be noted that a careful study of the writings of Innis, McLuhan and Grant, separately and in conjunction, thrusts us into the centre of a debate of world significance. For it is the gamble of the Canadian discourse on technology that, in disclosing the full horizon of the technological simulacrum within which we are trapped, and in revealing possibilities for transforming technique in the direction of human emancipation, Canadian thought partakes of the 20th century by posing the question of the human fate. In rethinking the meaning of Innis, McLuhan and Grant as the nodal points of the Canadian discourse we are also confronted with a more personal, and immediate, choice among lament, utopia, and political struggle as responses to the contemporary human condition. McLuhan once warned that we are being "x-rayed by television", and Grant noted that the fully technological society is populated by beings, "half-flesh, half-metal." What does this mean but that is our situation to be marooned, possibly with a very real exhaustion of political alternatives, in the processed world of high-technology. It was just this sense of the human exile *in* the technological world that represented, of course, the beginning-point for the thought of Harold Innis, George Grant, and Marshall McLuhan.

Technological Dependency: George Grant as the Nietzsche of the New World

Darkness in Civilization

A painting by the Canadian artist, Alex Colville, is a perfect text for reflecting upon the tragic vision of George Grant. Titled simply, if not deceptively, *To Prince Edward Island*, the painting is in the best of the realist tradition in North American art. This work is, in fact, almost severe in its simplicity; and the anxiety which it produces has less to do with any outward sign of trouble rising than with an eerie and vacant stillness which is its cumulative emotional effect. As always, Colville's artistic imagination concentrates on the particulars of the most prosaic events in order to show the depths of the darkness within.

The painting consists of two figures, a man and a woman, seated separately, with an almost geometric sense of estrangement, on the open deck of a boat. What is, immediately, most fascinating and disturbing about the work is the presence of a harsh contrast between the surface tranquillity of the seascape and the silence, tension, and hostility which are its inner language. There is, at first, the matter of the double exterminism which is portrayed in the painting. The man is a silenced presence, screened off by the muscular features of the woman, perfectly neutralized. And the woman? Her identity is also cancelled, and this purposively, by the presence of the binoculars. Indeed, the binoculars are the focal departure of the painting. They serve as both camouflage and screen. The vacant blue of the lenses, which liquidate the identity of the woman, are aggressive and menacing. We are as close as possible to the empty, and emotionally distressed, look of indifference which Gogol said would be the trademark of a society of "dead soul's." The binoculars block any reciprocity between the man and woman; and, for that matter, cancel out any possibility of human response between the woman and ourselves. It is as if the painting is about the human personality and thus identity itself, reduced to a flat "degree-zero."

There is in Colville's imagination a powerful, visual language of human deprivation, an authentically modern form of deprivation: produced not simply by domination from external sources, but by the coming into consciousness of the abyss of the void within. Only by means of a slight *trompe-l'oeil* can we notice the contrast between the surface realism of events and the "intimations of deprival" in the human figures. Consider, for example, the sharp contrasts everywhere in *To Prince Edward Island*. The sky is perfectly transparent and the sunlight brilliant, but there are *no* shadows in the paintings. The focus on the binoculars makes this work a study in looking, but what is most apparent is the perfect deadness of vision, and the sense that the woman, in inner desperation, is looking from nowhere to nothing. And always, although the painting is about motion (the boat) and communication (the two human figures), there is only an awful stillness and the impossibility of any human discourse. The sheer hyper-realism of the painting works to release, in fact, that which is just

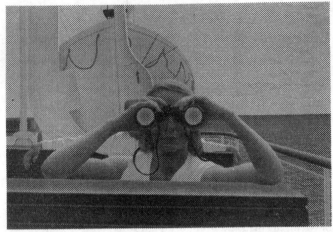

Alex Colville. *To Prince Edward Island*

beneath the surface: the suffocated scream of the woman; the signs everywhere of extreme, emotional distress; and the catastrophic sense of the impossibility of escape from the psychosis within. This, then, is a searing and unforgettable visual expression of inner madness which awaits only its moment of explosion. Colville tells us, and this directly, that, at the centre of the "modern project", all is doom, futility, and anguish: waiting with no expectation of relief; and looking with no possibility of response. As in all of Colville's work, from the terrifying and oppressive stillness of *Snow* to the melancholy psychosis of *Woman in a Bathtub* to the Goyaesque world of *Horse and Train*, it is the same: dead identities, dead vision, and an overwhelming sense of inner dread and anxiety. Colville is a North American existentialist: his paintings warn us that the crisis of modern civilization is not without, but integral to the human personality. It is in the area of the psychology of modern life that we come upon the human personality as its own asylum. In Colville's work, we are suddenly in the presence of the perfect freedom, the perfect anxiety, and also the coming darkness, of modern times.

To Prince Edward Island expresses in an austere and forbidding way the tragic insights achieved by George Grant into
the meaning of the unfolding of technological society as the
horizon of modern existence. Colville's artistic imagination
dwells on the detritus of modern society: human beings as
victims who, imprisoned in a social order which yields no
satisfactory response to the human demand for meaning, are
condemned to live in the desperate circumstances of a nihilistic
culture. Almost in primitive form, Colville's work hints of a
radically new type of dependency in the New World: a form of
human dependency which operates, not in the language of
sacrifice but of seduction; and which, not content to take
possession of the externals of the public order, now seeks to
colonize from within the being of these inhabitants of the
contemporary century. Colville is the artist who speaks directly
to the anxiety and bewilderment of an age haunted by an
overwhelming sense of the loss of some good fundamental to
the human spirit. And it is the very same with Grant's searing
vision of life in the "technological dynamo" of North America.
The irretrievable loss of some essential human good, only
hinted at in Colville's artistic productions, is the constant
subject-matter of Grant's philosophical imagination. Indeed,
Grant has generalized a "lament" over the human deprival
into a magisterial account of the inner workings of the technological order, and in an elegant, even loving, recovery of those
"precious aspects of experience" eliminated by the coming-
to-be of technique as the locus of the modern project. To the
"dead vision" at the centre of Colville's work, Grant responds
with the challenge that the task of inquiry today is to listen
intently for "intimations of deprival" which might suggest
ways of recovering a "more ancient account of the good"
against the "nihilistic will to will" of the technological
imperative.[1] This is to say that Grant is *ground* to Colville's
figure. Grant's thought moves at that critical, but elusive, edge
between the *realism* of the domain of actualities (the "modern,
technical system"), and the *absences* in that silent, invisible
universe of human deprival. That tenuous edge between the
wreckage of modern society and the remembrance of lost
possibilities is best captured in the blankness of the binoculars
at the centre of *To Prince Edward Island*. As if in this single image

the circle of modern dependency is closed: for what is this elimination of the "look" of the woman other than a sign of despair over the impossibility of an appeal to things past, and the awful knowledge that at the centre of things present, "nothingness spreads." Our suspension between an unbearable present and an irrecoverable past, between technology and mythology, is the elemental starting-point for Grant's reflections on damaged being in the fully modern society. In his inquiry, there is expressed, and in poetic form, most of the central themes of this tortured century: the present exhaustion and decadence of modern culture; the envelopment of North America within the "dynamic will to mastery" of the technological imperative;[2] the language of the drive to "planetary, technical future" as the primal of the New World;[3] the reduction of human experience to a servomechanism of the "technological dynamo"; and the suppressed hysteria of modern being at (our) knowledge of freedom in a "universe indifferent to what we choose."[4]

What the writer, John Berger, said of the artistic imagination of Picasso might also be said of Grant: his thought is that of a "vertical invader" who joins together in a common discourse the hidden sentiments of an anguished humanity, and an active, moral protest against the public reality of an abstract, and almost demonic, power. Grant is the Canadian philosopher who speaks directly to the emergence of the "darkness within" the deepest recesses of western civilization. In fact, it is not so much the nobility of Grant's words that is fascinating, as the pure wrath of his indictment of modern civilization. In Grant's discourse, there is gathered the full fury of a thinker, standing at the height of his times, who has taken careful measure of the calculus of the age, and who delivers a historical pronouncement on its fatal insufficiencies. Indeed, Grant stands closer to the more ancient practice of prophecy than to the narrow specialties of contemporary philosophical discourse. His words summon up in philosophy, once more, something of the nobility of its past traditions: a nobility which originates now, as it always has, with the commitment of a human life to the search for wisdom amidst the ruins of technological society, and to full engagement against the masters of human domination. With the synthetic vision of a modern prophet, Grant sees in North America the historical embodiment of a "pure will to technology."[5] There is in the technological dynamo only the celebration of a "nihilistic will to will": a celebration which marks a fundamental and irrecoverable shattering of any "adequate system of meaning" in the western tradition.[6] Against the "darkness which falls on the human will"[7] in the terrible nihilism of technological society, Grant's project is not so much a defence of tradition, but a desperate struggle to preserve some vestige of the dignity of human purpose, of a "human good", which is not reducible to consumer culture. That Grant's ruminations do not fit into traditional political categories is, perhaps, not so surprising. He is a socialist on the question of capital accumulation; a classical conservative in the domain of Canadian nationalism; an anarchist in the realm of the philosophical imagination; and a Christian on the meaning of social justice. He can practice only a proximate and relative politics just because his unforgiving vision of the "pure will to technology" as the primal impulse of North America is finally beyond the orthodox political discourse of the twentieth-century. Grant is indeed a prophet of the modern age.

Grant's intellectual contribution can be so paradoxical and his political legacy so equivocal just because all of his thought is deeply and constitutively religious. Indeed, an abiding concern with religion, understood in the broadest sense of the term, is the source of Grant's greatest strength and his biggest limit. It is his main advantage against the secular discourse of North America just because, as Grant himself once said, only religious experience has touched so persistently on the most profound themes of western civilization. Grant approaches the subject of technology like a Job of the New World. In his discourse, technological society is summoned to give its reasons before fundamental questions concerning the meaning of life and the possibility that evil, expressed in the abstract language of science and technology, is the locus of liberalism today. It's just because Grant's reflections on technology are so deeply embedded in a religious sensibility that he is able to provide such a charged historical account of the nihilism of modern culture. Paradoxically, however, the prophetic and tragic sense of Grant's thought is also the source of a great equivocation. More than is customary, his fundamentally religious temperament leaves no room for ·emancipatory politics or, for that matter, for any easy celebration of human creativity in the face of dismal odds. Grant's prejudices reflect accurately the discourse of the tory ego in North America: lamentation not emancipation; historical fatalism not collective political struggle; contemplation not engagement; and equivocation not pragmatism. The tragic turn in Grant's thought, so necessary to prophetic insight, and his privileging of mythic consciousness (natural law) over the political imagination screens out the real historical struggle of women and men in contemporary society. Just as the tragic sense of Grant's historicism cancels out the creative possibilities of the artistic imagination in going beyond technological dependency, so too his commitment to the religious viewpoint evacuates the gamble of politics in history. But then, if Grant's political legacy is so equivocal, this just means that better than most he has revealed the dark side of the bourgeois mind. Just like Nietzsche's *The Will to Power* and Adorno and Horkheimer's *The Dialectic of Enlightenment*, Grant is one of the "dark writers" of modern times. But, of course, Grant always had this advantage. As a Christian and a Loyalist of the Canadian, and thereby civil humanist variety, Grant is part of the founding tradition of modernity in North America. While Grant's ancestral roots in the Loyalist class in Canada may qualify him now only as a residual element within the dynamic and hegemonic culture of the "modern technical system", nonetheless it was the Loyalist contribution to flee to Canada (and continue their hegemony therewith) rather than surrender to the pragmatic implications of the American revolution. Two hundred years later, Grant on technology is the revenge of the United Empire Loyalists against the American dynamo. That Grant, a Christian and a classical nationalist can provide such critical insights into the nihilism of technological society may just prove that, today, in political philosophy as in quantum physics only contradictions are true.

Technology, Dependency and Power

To study Grant's writings on technology is to be drawn

into a compelling and masterful philosophy of civilization. Here is, in fact, a thinker who has meditated deeply upon, the meaning of technology as coeval with the spread of a new dark age of the human imagination. In his writings, the question of technology has been generalized into a sweeping, and critical, discourse on the crisis of modern society. This discourse moves from the most immediate, and intense, "lament" for the disappearance of Canadian nationalism to a more mediate, and abstract, reflection on the metaphysical origins of the disenchantment of western culture. His thought embraces simultaneously profound meditations on a vast arc of western thinkers (from the Athens-Jerusalem debate in Plato and Augustine to reflections on Marx and Weber) to searing, and satirical, political analysis of the "creative leadership" of technological society.[8] That Grant can move so easily from politics to philosophy, from poetic insight to historical conclusion, may be because his writings are only variations on a common theme. He is the North American thinker who has explored, with the greatest intensity and eloquence, the limits of dependent being in technological society.

Grant is, in fact, the Nietzsche of the New World. In *The Will to Power*, that fundamental reflection on the nihilism of European culture, Nietzsche spoke of the envelopment of human experience within the closed horizon of a society, driven from within by a relentless "will to will." Nietzsche situated dependency in the reduction of the human project — work, ethics, reason, identity, *all* of the major loci of human reality — to the servicing of a restless and empty "will to power" at the centre of things.[9] For Nietzsche, the "new world" began with the pure will to technique, indeed with the abstract and demonic will to accumulation *and* disintegration, as the dynamic locus of the modern account of itself. In Nietzsche's unforgettable words, with the unfolding of the "will", of *technique* itself, as the nucleus of the secular age, "the horizon had finally been wiped clean."[10] Long in advance of the present century, with its despair over human impotence in the face of power and technology, Nietzsche knew that a new, and intensified, version of technical domination was being prepared for the inhabitants of the empire of technology. He also recognized, tragically so, that with the coming-to-be of the society of the pure drive to technique, there could be no turning back to the recovery, however urgent, of the "inner restraints" of western culture. Long before the term became fashionable in intellectual discourse, Nietzsche was a dependency theorist; and this in the most serious sense. He described the inner movements of a nightmarish world in which human beings were reduced to the "commandments" of the will to technique.[11] Nietzsche intimated that the most intense, and impossible, form of human dependency lay in the narrowing of the human identity into a living instrument of the will to power. He could thus say of the will to mastery as the inner dynamic of the "modern project" that it was *not* different from us. The peculiar tragedy of the modern fate is that we would be compelled to live within the "horizon" of technological society as one of its instruments.

Writing from the perspective of the twentieth- as opposed to the nineteenth-century, and from the Great Lakes region of North America and not European society, Grant continues anew Nietzsche's meditation on the limitlessness of human domination in the "technological dynamo". In a short essay titled, "A Platitude", a work which is Grant's most existential reflection on technology as dependency, Grant states: "We can hold in our minds the enormous benefits of technological society, but we cannot so easily hold the ways it may have deprived us, *because technique is ourselves*."[12] Grant's thought moves and plays in that region of the most terrible of truths: the full penetration of technique, the will to mastery, into the deepest interstices of human personality. The analysis represents a brilliant psychology of the human condition: it discloses a suffocating vision of life within the "modern, technical system" as the secret of dependent being in the "unlimited" and "functional" universe of technology and science. And there is more: "All descriptions or definitions of technique which place it outside ourselves hide from us what it is."[13] Grant is unrelenting. Perhaps even more than Nietzsche, he insists on showing that the dynamic momentum of technology is integral to the modern myth; that, in fact, we cannot so easily escape responsibility for the spreading of the technological imperative as the very charisma, the past and future hope, of North America. "Technique comes forth and is sustained in our vision of ourselves as creative freedom, making ourselves, and conquering the chaos of an indifferent universe."[14] This is only to note what is most paradoxical and ambivalent about the question of technology. The powers and dominations of technology work in the name of "creative freedom"; the justification for an unlimited expansion of the technical order has its roots deep in the archeology of western consciousness; and the very language of "technical advance" is cosubstantial with the approved vocabulary of the maximization of "values" in the personal and public realms. Again, "technique is ourselves"; and it is so in a way that is fully internal to the self-understanding of the modern project. For Grant, as for Nietzsche before him, dependency is no longer a matter of the externalities of human experience; but involves a radical colonization *from within* of the psychology of the modern self. "All coherent languages beyond those which serve the drive to unlimited freedom through technique have been broken up in the coming to be of what we are. Therefore it is impossible to articulate publicly any suggestion of loss, and perhaps even more frightening, almost impossible to articulate it to ourselves."[15] The frenzied drive to "freedom through technique"[16] is, in a word, the *horizon* of modern culture. And as with any horizon which serves, after all, to envelop the human project in a coherent system of meaning, we can never be certain of our ability to think against and beyond the horizon of technical reason. The ambivalence of technological reason as the almost *metaphorical* structure of human domination is this: even as we live within the horizon of technological society, we may have been dispossessed of any "language of the good" by which to measure the present catastrophe. This is the true limit of human dispossession: the stripping away from the inhabitants of the New World of the ability to preserve if only in memory, a real difference between the propaganda of the "drive to planetary technical future", and the now dead speech of "some good necessary to man as man". What the critical theorist, Theodor Adorno, once described as the "historical amnesia"[17] of advanced industrial societies, Grant would typify as (our) forgetfulness of the "intimations of deprival" by which the horizon of the historical age might be breached. In the terrifying words which the poet, Dennis Lee, directed to the disintegration of the Canadian identity, but which might also be said of Grant's understanding of modern dispossession: "Silence is the colonial cadence."[18]

But Grant is, yet, even more precise on the conditions of our incarceration in the prison-house of technology. For if it is Grant's *historical* thesis that North Americans share in a privileged way in the unfolding of technological experience, then it is also his *existential* insight that the limits of human deprival are now approached in the "fanaticism" of the "spearhead of modernity", the United States. In a seminal essay, "In Defence of North America", Grant could say that "... to exist as a North American is an amazing and enthralling fate."[19] And this is so because the United States is the first fully modern society: the society in which Hegel's terrible vision of the "universal and homogenous state" was suddenly transposed from theoretical possibility into historical actuality. In Grant's sense, the New World has always been a radical experiment in giving concrete, material expression to the *idea* of (our) creative freedom to transform the world as we choose. The primal of North America, in its religion, economy, and culture, has been, and this continually, the fantastically pragmatic will to make good on the possibility that this is the "promised land of the realized technological society."[20] And yet is not the coming fate, and peril, of the New World that we now live in the detritus of hi-tech? "An unlimited freedom to make the world as we want in a universe indifferent to what purpose we choose."[21] The "dynamic expansion" of the technocratic imperative, which in Grant's sense is also and always the spread of the "will to will", can have no absolute limit. This is why he recurs time and again to the image of space flight with its explicit disavowal of any *intrinsic* purpose as an almost chilling example that, perhaps, the "fully realized technological society" has passed beyond another threshold in its nihilism. Indeed, Grant can speak of the American space programme in terms of the production of "beings, half-flesh, half-metal"[22] because, in its absence of an instrinsic justification, we discover a new high-point in the limitlessness of "creative freedom" in an indifferent universe. The ultimate consequence of the "unlimited expansion" of the technocratic system is just what Grant says, and it is haunting: individuals in modernity are compelled to live in a "divided state":

> . . . the plush patina of hectic subjectivity lived out in the iron maiden of an objectified world inhabited by increasingly objectifiable beings.[23]

Yet the conclusion of "A Platitude", there is a wonderful insight which might represent a path out of the present darkness. (Grant is a political realist of the most bitter order.)

> . . . all languages of good except the language of the drive to freedom have disintegrated, so it is just to pass some antique wind to speak of goods that belong to man as man. Yet the answer is always the same: if we cannot so speak, then we can either only celebrate or stand in silence before that drive. Only in listening for the intimations of deprival can we live critically in that dynamo.[24]

Grant provides this important clue for, if not an exit from, then at least a way of "living critically" in, the darkness of the contemporary century. "Any intimations of authentic deprival are precious, because they are ways through which intimations of good, unthinkable in public terms, may yet appear to us."[25] Now as always we have an inescapable moral choice which derives from our direct implication in the human circumstance: "working for or celebrating the dynamo" or "listening or watching or simply waiting for intimations of deprival which might lead us to see the beautiful as the image, in the world, of the good."[26] Grant writes in the language of deprival as, perhaps, the only way open to us of recovering a new, and more substantive, image of the human situation. When technique is thought and lived as a dependency relation fully integral to the human personality; that is, when "we" are technique, then Grant instructs us that any movement which seeks to transcend the horizon of the technocratic imperative must begin, and can only begin, with a reformation of human identity. It is also the fundamentals of human psychology which are wagered in this struggle with the "drive to mastery'. of technological society.

The Double Refusal

The compelling quality of Grant's critique of the technocratic imperative is that his thought is informed by a double refusal of the "modern project": a refusal which is, at once, historical and ontological.*

Grant's "historical refusal" is coeval with the tory touch in Canadian politics: with that part of Canadian political discourse which began, and in its best but most marginal features, now continues as a radical repudiation of the "liberal experiment" that was the United States in the age of progress. This is to say that Grant's ancestory may be traced directly to the Loyalists, and consequently to their great refusal of the American Revolution, and with it, of all the deep assumptions of the modern project. Grant, then, is the philosophical exponent of a "dying class" in Canada: he speaks for a fully marginal element in the Canadian political experience, an element which to survive can only reconcile itself with the dominant assumptions of technological society by giving its public loyalties (as part of the ruling class) to the "creative leadership" of the liberal experiment. But as Barrington Moore once intimated, the peculiar nobility of any dying class, of a class which has no future sinecure in the pragmatic blast of history, is that its membership is sometimes finally free to articulate one last, elegaic, and disinterested vision of human freedom.[27] This is just what Grant has done.

What accounts for the continuing magnetism of his

---

* Grant's refusal of the "modern project" is, in its essentials, a rejection *tout court* of the politics and deep philosophical assumptions of liberalism. His refusal of liberalism is *ontological* just to the extent that it moves beyond a direct, political criticism of the instrumental activism of American empire to a sustained reflection on the *theory of being* which is, at once, the necessary condition for and consequence of liberalism today. This is a meditation from the centre of the culture of nihilism.

thought, for the remarkable fact that his perspective on technology as dependency serves as a gravitational-point around which coalesced a politically divergent group, including Patricia Marchak, Daniel Drache, and James Laxer, is precisely the *probity* of his inquiry. Grant's mind is scathing and satirical. More than is customary, he outrages the liberal sensibility in Canadian thought by noting, time and again, the betrayal of the possibility that was Canada by the "bureaucratic leadership" of the liberal discourse. Grant's thought holds Canadian liberalism in contempt, a cow-catcher for American empire: the Canadian elite, "the established wealthy of Montréal and Toronto, who had once seen themselves the pillars of Canada", and the "international bureaucracy", from Mackenzie King to C.D. Howe, Pearson, and Trudeau, who actively allied themselves with the "capitalist liberalism of the United States" and "who lost nothing essential to the principles of their lives in losing their country".[28] Against the betrayal of Canadian nationalism by a liberal elite which had deeply absorbed the "animating vision" of American culture, Grant says simply:

> The impossibility of conservatism in our era is the impossibility of Canada. As Canadians we attempted a ridiculous task in trying to build a conservative nation in the age of progress, on a continent shared with the most dynamic nation on earth. The current of modern history was against us.[29]

Grant's nationalism is emancipatory, a critical defence of "local cultures" and a scatological critique of capitalism as the deep moral rot of modern society. "No small country can depend for its existence on the loyalty of its capitalists. International interests may require the sacrifice of the lesser loyalty of patriotism. Only in dominant nations is the loyalty of capitalists ensured. In such situations, their interests are tied to the strength and vigour of their empire."[30] Grant's nationalism is crafted against a political landscape dominated by the capitalism of the American way. His special insight was to immediately grasp the "levelling effect" of capitalist liberalism. Indeed, Grant can say that "indigenous cultures are dying everywhere in the modern world", because the spread of "dynamic civilization" requires the absorption of all local energies into the bland, institutional imperatives of the "technological dynamo".[31] For English-Canada, this meant the disappearance of the "inner restraint", that peculiar derivative of Canada's continuing discourse with the classical origins of culture in Europe, and the gradual "unleashing of unrestrained passions"[32] as the psychological sign of admission to American empire. And Québec, the last and best hope for an "indigenous alternative" to technological civilization? "As traditional Catholicism breaks up, there will be some exciting moments. A Catholic society cannot be modernized as easily as a Protestant one. When the dam breaks the flood will be furious. Nevertheless, the young intellectuals of the upper-middle class will gradually desert their existentialist nationalism and take places made for them in the continental corporations."[33] For Grant, the future of Québec is that of existential despair. "The enormity of the break from the past will arouse in the dispossessed youth intense forms of beatness."[34] But this is not dissent, only political compromise: on the one hand, "a majority of the young is gradually patterned for its place in the bureaucracies;" and on the other, those who resist will "retreat into a fringe world of pseudo-revolt."[35] But even pseudo-revolt has a greater nobility of purpose than the happy acquiescence of English-Canada in the ideology of continentalism. English-Canada is the society of Nietzsche's "last men": people "who have never learned to despise themselves" and thus say "consumption is good", and blink.[36] For Québec is reserved the terrible night of nihilism which comes with the disintegration of Catholicism, and with the certain knowledge that the "dynamic civilization" of the United States can provide only a deeply compromised vision of the good life.

Grant's "historical refusal" thus culminates in a philosophical nationalism, a love of the Canadian possibility as both a "love of one's own" and a precious recovery of a lost image of the "human good." The Canadian possibility was always only as a cultural alternative to the expansionary liberal vision of the United States. This is an order of nationalism simultaneously regional and cosmopolitan: at one polarity, an almost mournful appeal for the recovery of popular culture, for the activation of "memory" itself as a form of political resistance to empire, yet at the other, fully universal in embracing any moment of cultural resistance which represents a refusal of the "uniform, world culture"[37] of capitalist liberalism. It is, in fact, Grant's defence of Canada as an "alternative culture",[38] and of Québec as an "indigenous culture"[39] in North America whose fate in entangled with thinking outside of and against the abstract power of "dynamic civilization" which issues, with compelling and original force, in the form of a "lament." Grant is a complete thinker to the extent that he has pioneered the method of the "lament" as the literary, and philosophical, expression most adequate for conveying the tragic quality of his historical refusal. In *Lament for a Nation*, Grant remarked that "to lament is to cry out at the death or at the dying of something loved. This lament mourns the end of Canada as a sovereign state."[40] In "Canada's disappearance" before the "technological dynamo," Grant said that there was also the passing away of a civilization which might have "served the good;" which might, with Québec, have built an "ordered and stable society" as an alternative to the liberal experiment of the United States."[41] But now there can only be the keening of lament in the face of the "homogenized culture of the American Empire." "A lament arises from a condition that is common to the majority of men, for we are situated between despair and absolute certainty."[42] And thus, Grant's historical refusal makes "no practical proposals for our survival as a nation."[43] It results only in a tragic lament, a "celebration of memory": "the tenuous memory that was the principle of my ancestors".

But Grant's lament, while pessimistic, is not fatalistic. In *Philosophy in the Mass Age*, Grant remarked of the human passion for change in the face of great injustice: "To those who are not so reconciled, the sense of meaninglessness should not result in a beaten retirement, but in a rage for action."[44] Why? Grant says that Jean-Paul Sartre is the "clearest of modern humanists" because he understood the indispensable connection between pessimism and freedom: "Real pessimism must surely lead to the active life and the affirmation of human freedom."[45] This may be why Grant's "lament", this authentic meditation on "Canada's disappea-

rance" may also be a call to action. The pessimism is overwhelming:

> We find ourselves like fish left on the shores of a drying
> lake. The element necessary to our existence has passed
> away. As some form of political loyalty is part of the good
> life, and as we are not flexible enough to kneel to the rising
> sun, we must be allowed to lament the passing of what had
> claimed our allegiance. Even on a continent too dynamic to
> have memory, it may still be saluatory to celebrate memory.
> The history of the race is strewn with gasping political
> fish.[46]

But if Grant's pessimism is real, then so also is the "tenuous
hope" which it inspires. Grant can speak of the disintegration
of the "indigenous culture" that was Canada as somehow
removing a last barrier on the road to the "tyranny of the
universal and homogenous state." And he can do so because
he equates the Canadian fate, this struggle on a minor note
between a small, local culture and the "dynamo" of the
modern, technical system, as but the passing reflection of a
much greater *ontological* struggle. Grant tells us that what is at
stake in our confrontation with the "American way" is a
momentous and decisive philosophical struggle between two
opposing ways of being: the nihilism of modern being; and the
recovery of a more authentic way of being in the traditional
practices of a more ancient account of justice. Just as Grant's
"lament" is midway between the "propositions of the saints"
and the "absolute despair" of the poets, so too his "historical
refusal," which is based on a tragic account of Canada's
dependent state in the New World, is midway between politics
and philosophy.[47] Where others only saw what was proximate
and apparent in the discourse of the New World, Grant
recognized the clear and unmistakeable signs of the reappea-
rance, in North America, of a more elemental philosophical
struggle in the western mind. Grant grasped continuously
what that was really going on in North America, in the bitter
struggles between the American Empire and its peripheries in
Québec, Mexico, and English-Canada, was a fundamental
contest over the direction of western ontology. The flash-
point of Grant's thought remains his "historical refusal" of

the seductions of technological civilization, as exemplified most intensely by the United States. Indeed, *In Philosophy in the Mass Age*, he remarked that the Great Lakes region of North America is the "chief creative centre" from which spreads out the "driving will to mastery" of technological society.[48] But Grant's denial of the "affirmations" and "affluence" of the will to technology only breaks ground for another, more decisive, negation: an "ontological refusal" of the modern project itself. What began in *Lament for a Nation* as a specific, political meditation on the defeat of John Diefenbaker (a "bewildered," but authentic, nationalist) at the hands of a new class alliance between the Canadian liberal elite and its "American masters," is quickly generalized into powerful, philosophical criticism of the central themes of technological civilization. That Grant can slide so easily between historical and philosophical criticism, (between, that is, bitter political analysis and an almost detached philosophy of civilization) may be due to the fact that his thought discloses a new threshold in the New World mind.

The implication of Grant's "double refusal" (both of the *immediate* imperialism of the United States, and of the more *mediate* categories of western civilization within which the "pure will to technique" of the American way is couched) is this. If the "technological dynamo" of the United States brings to perfect fruition the "nihilistic will to will" of a now exhausted European culture; if North America has been the brilliant, historical vanguard of the "modern project": then New World thinkers cannot escape the hidden side, the dark side, of their participation, either at the centre or the peripheries, in the "most fully modern society"[49] in western civilization. For better or for worse, the politics and philosophy of the New World are privileged: they represent, by virtue of historical circumstance, the forward edge for the working-out of the basic formula of the western mind. It is precisely this fateful encounter of politics and ontology in the New World mind which is given such powerful expression in Grant's thought. Perhaps even against his own, more limited, intentions, Grant's "historical refusal" is only the vertical grounding for a fundamental and coherent philosophical criticism of the epistemology, aesthetics, morality, and politics of the "modern

project." At its most profound level, his criticism of technological dependency is expressed in the sometimes ironic,
always bitter, language of ontology. While this confrontation
of Grant's mind with the politics, and then the ontology, of
technological dependency reveals the full depths of human
domination in the New World (and by extension everywhere
now in the "universal culture" of capitalist liberalism), it also
marks a great rupture in the western mind. For the gamble of
Grant's thought lies in the fact that if the nihilism of technology drags us to the limits of domination, and this in a last,
hysterical plunge into a cycle of exterminism, then there is
also another possibility. Amidst the ruins of North America,
after all, only the unfolding of the "disaster" in the western
mind, we might just discover a new philosophical, and then
historical, possibility. The New World mind breaks both ways
now: towards the exterminism of western civilization at the
hands of "technological liberalism";[50] and, in the desperation
of our historical circumstances, to the search for some
restorative of the nobler instincts in western culture for the
conduct of public, and private, affairs. The New World stands,
now as always, at high noon between the dead present of
technological society and the unknown future of some
account of the "human good" which would reassert the
connection of justice and technology. The violence of the
New World is a sure sign of the presence of a warring ontology
in the modern mind: a philosophical, and then political,
division which, running like a great seismic fracture across the
discourse of the New World, separates it into either a privileged participant in the "dynamic willing" of technological
society, or a witness to the "daybreak" of a new social order.
This silent, but vast, division between the totality of the
"modern project" and the emergent signs of a new cultural
practice, this struggle between justice and technology, is the
locus of Grant's ontological refusal. In his estimation, the
fantastic, and perhaps unbridgeable, gap between the power
of the technical apparatus and the critical promise contained
in the "deprivals" of technological society means that we live
in a situation of the "either/or." Indeed, Grant describes this
great divide in modern existence as a "civilizational contradiction."

For the last centuries a civilizational contradiction has moved our western lives. Our greatest intellectual endeavour — the new co-penetration of 'logos' and 'techne' — affirmed that in understanding everything we know it as ruled by necessity and chance. This affirmation entailed the elimination of the ancient notion of good from the understanding of anything. At the same time, our day-to-day organization was in the main directed by a conception of justice formulated in relation to the ancient science, in which the notion of good was essential to the understanding of what is. This civilizational contradiction arose from the attempt of the articulate to hold together what was then given in modern science with a content of justice which had been developed out of an older account of what is.[51]

Technological Liberalism

Grant's double refusal of the technocratic imperative — his *historical* denial of the moral propriety of the American way, and his *ontological* criticism of the way of being endemic to the empire of technique — culminates in a despairing vision of the "language of willing"[52] as the dynamic matrix of North America. Grant is unrelenting in his insistence that *all* aspects of technological society are reducible to a common source, the language of will. It is, in fact, the "meeting of reasoning and willing in the western mind"[53] and the consequent abolition of all modes of thought and action not supportive of "willing" which is the dynamic momentum at the centre of modern existence. Time and again, Grant states that his purpose has been to undertake an "enucleation of the modern project." "The word 'enucleation' implies that I am not simply interested in describing the manifestations of that vision, for example the mastery of movement through space or the control of heredity. . . . In another age, it would have been proper to say that I am attempting to partake in the soul of modernity."[54] Grant's "partaking" in the spirit of modernity has resulted in a comprehensive, and thematically unified, account of the human situation. What congeals his discourse, and what makes of Grant's account of the central foundations of technological society such a remarkable treatise on the "animating vision" of contemporary society, is this. More than he may have realized, Grant has succeeded in "enucleating" the modern project. In his different texts, there is to be found an internally coherent and persuasive demonstration that the epistemology (positivist), political theory (liberal), public morality (instrumental activism), category of time (historical), vision of history (progressivist), aesthetics (contractarianism), social relations (competitive), value-principle (pragmatism), and psychology (nihilistic) — all of the "foundational categories"[55] of the modern project — are but derivative expressions of that which is most central to western experience: the language of willing. In his diverse reflections on the "will" as the secret kernel of technological society, Grant may have stumbled upon the DNA of modern society. For he has reinterpreted the question of technology in terms of (our) incarceration in a power-system which is, at once, abstract, disembodied, and reductionist. Grant instructs us that the limits of human dispossession go beyond the "surface manifestations" of technique, to a deeper and more intractable impoverishment of the human spirit. In his most tormented writing, *Time as History*, Grant has says of our disempowerment in technological society:

> Our present is like being lost in the wilderness, where every pine and rock and bay appears to us as both known and unknown, and therefore as uncertain pointers on the way back to human habitation. The sun is hidden by the clouds and the usefulness of our ancient compasses has been put into question. Even what is beautiful — has been made equivocal for us both in detail and definition.[56]

Everything in Grant's thought revolves around a central, intellectual theme: an urgent effort on his part to understand the hidden sources of the nihilism in western society; or, what is the same, to comprehend the full meaning of technique as the "will to will." *Philosophy in the Mass Age* is a fundamental, epistemological reflection on the will to truth (and freedom) as the necessary philosophical basis of the coming-to-be of the technological world-view. In this text, Grant traces the birth of the "modern technical system" to a great scission in the western tradition between "mythic" and "modern" consciousness. Grant's most basic methodological claim is that the meaning of technological society can only be disclosed by means of a critical understanding of the "all-encompassing world-view" which is embodied in and carried forward under the name of technology. Grant is not so much preoccupied with technology as "moon-shots" or "automated machinery", but rather as a certain angle of vision which has been brought to bear on western experience as its central organizational principle. This "expansive" interpretation of technology is central to his distinction between mythic and modern consciousness as the condition of possibility of the "modern technical system". For it is Grant's contention that technological society rests on a series of *exlusions* (religious morality, mythic consciousness, natural law, the tragic imagination); and a series of *actualizations* (pragmatic morality, historical consciousness, positive law, and instrumental reasoning). All of *Philosophy in the Mass Age* represents an intense and thorough exploration of that great rupture in the western mind which resulted in our abandonment of "mythic consciousness,"[57] and the privileging in the modern age of an aggressive, but bankrupt, vision of historical activism as freedom. Grant remarks that it has been the "destiny of western European peoples to be the first to destroy their old religious society and to replace it with modern scientific culture . . . ."[58] But, the essential difference between contemporary society and "the old is not only, or even primarily, the external difference shown by our mastery over nature through science and technology, but a profound difference in man's very view of himself."[59] Having rejected "mythic consciousness", we see ourselves "rather as the makers of history, the makers of our own laws. We are authentically free since nothing beyond us limits what we should do."[60] This is the essential theme: having adopted modern consciousness we are condemned "to freedom in a universe indifferent to our purposes";[61] and having denied "mythic consciousness," we have also abandoned Plato's vision of "time as a moving image of eternity."[62] Grant laments the passing of the Greek imagination, at least in its tragic aspects, as the informing impulse of western civilization.

Grant's reflections on the radical implications of the break-up in western culture of "mythic" and "modern" consciousness continues in *English-Speaking Justice*. While *Philosophy in the*

Mass Age brought to a new height of intellectual expression the *epistemological* claims necessary for the upsurge of the "technical age", *English-Speaking Justice* examines the *aesthetic* assumptions of technological society. In this text, Grant expands on his general thesis of a fundamental irreconcilability between justice and technology; or, what is the same the impossibility for a "substantive" as opposed to purely "conventional and contractual" conception of justice to be incorporated into the public morality of technological society. Grant strips away the ethical veneer of the technical age, only to reveal that in the meeting of "contractual liberalism" and the technocratic imperative, there is produced an account of justice which reduces itself to the pursuit of "primary goods." In its political formulation, this would mean that the modern account of justice in the "advanced liberal society" results in a fantastic reduction of the ends of public (or private) justice to the organization of society around "human conveniences which fit the conveniences of technology."[63] Whereas in the western tradition "justice in human relationships was the essential way in which human beings are opened to eternity"[64] and this (substantive) conception of justice implied an intimate connection between "inward" and "outward" justice, in the modern account there is only a great, and unalterable, division between inward and outward justice.

The chief contribution of *English-Speaking Justice* is as an exploration of the "inner bankruptcy" in the modern (liberal) account of justice: both in the sense that "contractual liberalism" cannot provide a suitable answer to what we are "fit for" now that the ends of the "technological endeavour" have been reduced to mass consumption of "primary goods"; and, to the extent, that the modern version of justice cannot reconcile the more ancient "content" of liberty and equality with the formal requirements of the technical system to "expand" at all costs, and this in the name of the "greater conveniences." That Grant has succeeded in seeing straight through to the "darkness within" the liberal account of justice ("liberalism ... belongs to the flesh and bones of our institutions")[65] may be because his inquiry first links contractual liberalism and technology as emerging from the "same matrix of modern thought."

Nevertheless, it must be stated that our justice now moves to a lowered content of equal liberty. The chief cause of this is that our justice is being played out within a destiny more comprehensive than itself. A quick name for this is 'technology'. I mean by that word the endeavour which summons forth everything (both human and non-human) to give its reasons and through the summoning forth of those reasons turns the world into potential raw material, at the disposal of our "creative wills."[66]

Now, the specific mark of Grant's meditation on the antithesis of justice and technology is that it fuses a political and metaphysical analysis of this relationship. As a political diagnosis, *English-Speaking Justice* can hardly be surpassed. Speaking satirically of the "creative leaders in the corporations", Grant says that having been told "for many generations that justice is only a convenience", why should they, in "carrying out the dynamic conveniences of technology ... not seek a justice which is congruent with those conveniences, and gradually sacrifice the principles of liberty and equality when they conflict with the greater conveniences."[67] And Grant can quote Huey Long's dictum, "When fascism comes to America, it will come in the name of democracy,"[68] because he understands precisely what is involved in the movement to "large-scale equality" under the tutelage of the "creative" leaders of technological society.

In such a situation, equality in 'primary goods' for a majority in the heartlands of the empire is likely; but it will be an equality which excludes liberal justice for those who are inconvenient to the 'creative.' It will exclude liberal justice for those who are too weak to enforce contracts — the imprisoned, the mentally unstable, the unborn, the aged, the defeated, and sometimes even the morally unconforming.[69]

"Injustice for the very weak" is the political price to be paid for the unfolding of the technical age as the broader destiny of the liberal account of justice. If, however, the political analysis of *English-Speaking Justice* discloses a grim, and mean-spirited, reduction of public justice to a question of power in technological society, then the metaphysical diagnosis of the crisis is even more shattering. For it is Grant's thesis that the savage politics of "contractual liberalism" is an inevitable expression of a deeper logic of nihilism in the western mind. Grant is adamant in his insistence that the "contractarian tradition" in western thought, a tradition which is given its most complete and contemporary expression in John Rawls' *A Theory of Justice* but which has its origins in Kant's *The Critique of Pure Reason*, contains a fatal contradiction. Grant follows Nietzsche in saying of Kant that he is "the great delayer";[70] indeed, that Kant's thought is "the consummate expression of wanting it both ways."[71] In Grant's estimation, it was Kant's outstanding contribution to the contemporary theory of justice to allow "generations of intellectuals" the false comfort that they could keep, and this simultaneously, both the assumptions of "technological secularism" and the "absolutes of the old morality."[72] Kant sought to preserve a dynamic harmony between an ancient account of justice and the unlimited freedom to be found in the "will to make one's own life."[73] Kant's description of the "morally good will" as the basis of the just society is, consequently, the locus of an uneasy compromise in the western mind. It represents the basic philosophical formula by which the exponents of the social-contract tradition, this latter-day expression of "secularised Christianity", will seek to escape the full consequences of modern consciousness. But for Grant, following Nietzsche, the contemporary era is fully relativist and historicist. There can be no adequate modern account of what justice is because " . . . once we have recognized 'history' as the imposing of our wills on an accidental world," then justice is only the other side of nihilism.[74] Kant's "delaying" tactic was thus essential.

> Having understood what is told us about nature in our science, and having understood that we will and make our own history, he turned away from the consequence of those recognitions by enfolding them in the higher affirmation that morality is the one fact of reason, and we are commanded to obedience. According to Nietzsche, he limited autonomy by obedience.[75]

Kant is at the centre of the "civilisational contradiction" which will come to plague technological society from the inside. As Grant says, in the essence of his critique of the liberal account of justice:

> He delayed them from knowing that there are no moral facts, but only the moral interpretations of facts, and that these interpretations can be explained as arising from the historical vicissitudes of the senses. Moral interpretations are what we call our 'values', and these are what our wills impose upon the facts.[76]

Everything follows from Grant's fateful decision to see the nihilism in Kant: a scathing critique of Rawl's *A Theory of Justice*, not only as the penultimate expression of "American bourgeois common-sense," but as an outstanding example of the failure of liberal political theory to produce a substantive conception of public, and private, justice; an agonizing reflection on the impossibility of recognizing, in the midst of the "necessity and chance" of modern science, the essential lineaments of "what justice is"; and the despairing insight that in this time of "great darkness" it is the human predicament not to be able to return to an "ancient account of justice as if the discoveries of the modern science of nature had not taken place", nor to surrender the question of "what it means to say that justice is what we are fitted for."[77] And, more ironically, as we live this "civilisational contradiction" in the pragmatic unfolding of the New World, we cannot rely on the philosophical wisdom of the English political moralists. And here, Grant is most satiricial. In speaking of the liberal tradition among English-speaking peoples, a tradition which finds its enucleation in Mill and Russell, Grant says that they failed to devise some conception of the political good which might now protect us from the "possibility of technological tyranny."[78] In a bitter commentary in *English-Speaking Justice*, Grant remarks that while "there are worse things than a nation of shopkeepers," this traditional consensus "about political good, and the resulting poverty of thought, did much to innoculate the English from those theoretical viruses which have plagued continental Europeans."[79] The very philosophical poverty of the English "protected them from its modern extremities" while also leaving them "singularly unprepared to understand the extremities of the twentieth century."[80] Thus the paradox: the liberal account of justice develops out of an (English) theoretical tradition which suffers radical amnesia on the political implications of modern justice; and it is politically implemented in an (American) constitutional tradition which is oblivious to the metaphysical reasons for the "great darkness" within the pragmatic conception of the just society.

If *English-Speaking Justice* discloses the philosophical basis for the unfolding of technological society in a coarse and brutal language of power, then it does so through the brilliant expedient of bringing Nietzsche's reflections on the "will to power" to bear on the question of liberal justice. Nowhere, however, is the Nietzschean side of Grant's mind more in evidence than in his most mature writing, *Time as History*. This text represents a grand summational statement of all of the enduring themes in Grant's discourse on technology: the insight that technology is the embodiment of modern nihilism; the recognition that the limits of human dependency have been achieved when we can say, "technique is ourselves"; the calculus of "reasoning and willing" as the nucleus of the "dynamic spirit" of the New World; and the (historical) observation that the importance of North America, particularly in the heartland of the empire, derives from its representing in an advanced political form that rudimentary code of the modern mind — the "pure will to technique" as the essence of human freedom. In *Time as History*, there is an active, and magisterial, synthesis of the whole range of Grant's writings: from the essays which comprised *Technology and Empire* and the meditation of *Lament for a Nation* to the more specific philosophical reflections of *Philosophy in the Mass Age* and *English-Speaking Justice*. And *Time as History* serves as Grant's major, synthetic statement on the question on technology because it contains a formidable and comprehensive phenomenology of the modern mind. In this writing, nothing is spared. For perhaps the first time since Nietzsche's account of the modern project in *The Will to Power*, Grant reverses the usual critique of technology by compelling us to examine the deep implication of the western mind and of the modern personality in the development of technological society. This is a bitter, and entirely honest, exploration of barbarism in the modern age.

Grant's absorption, and highly original application to North America, of the thought of Nietzsche is explicit.

> I have brushed against the writings of Nietzsche because he has thought the conception of time as history more comprehensively than any other thinker. He lays bare the fate of technical man, not as an object held in front of us, but as that in which our very selves are involved in the proofs of the science which lays it bare. In thinking the modern project, he did not turn away from it.
>
> In his work, the themes that must be thought in thinking time as history are raised to a beautiful explicitness: the mastery of human and non-human nature in experimental science and technique, the primacy of the will, man as the creator of his own values, the finality of becoming, the assertion that potentiality is higher than actuality, that motion is nobler than rest, that dynamism rather than peace is the height.[81]

In perhaps his most haunting, and decisive, statement on the new dark spirit in western civilization, Grant notes that a culture of nihilism is the most likely outcome of the great divide in modern mind between justice and technology, and between meaning and technique. In *Time as History*, Grant remarks that last men and nihilists are everywhere in North America today. "The last men will gradually come to be the majority in any realized technical society."[82] For Grant, a society of "last men" is inevitable since this is the psychological fall-out from the urgent quest for liberty and equality in the age of progress.

> The central fact about the last men is that they cannot despise themselves. Because they cannot despise themselves, they cannot rise beyond a petty view of happiness. They can thus inoculate themselves against the abyss of existing. They are the *last* men because they have inherited rationalism only in its last and decadent form.[83]

And the nihilist? Here Grant is fully faithful to Nietzsche's pronouncements on the "cataclyms and violence" which will attend the final days of the strong, the "creative leaders,"[84] in their will to mastery. It is the special balm of "last men" that the "little they ask of life (only entertainment) will give them endurance." Not so though for the nihilists.

> These are those who understand that they can know nothing about what is good to will. Because of the historical sense, they know that all values are relative and man-made; the highest values of the past have devalued themselves . . . But because men are wills, the strong cannot give up willingly. *Men would rather will nothing then have nothing to will.*[85]

With this profound understanding of technological society as directed, in the end, by the "creative" who would "rather will nothing" than not will at all, Grant achieves an almost luminous insight into the psychology of modern life. For what can motivate last men and nihilists other than, as Nietzsche had already said, the loosing of a "howling spirit of revenge"[86] in the New World. But the modern "spirit of revenge" is of a particular sort. It is born in the specific despair, and anguish, of knowing ourselves to be *wills* in a world devoid of meaning. It has as its objects the "will to revenge against others, against ourselves, against the very condition of time itself."[87] And the "spirit of revenge" continues in this (psychological) form: "The more botched and bungled our instincts become in the vicissitudes of existing, the greater our will to revenge on what has been done to us."[88] For Nietzsche, and later for Grant, it is the "will to revenge" which is the psychological horizon of the fully realized technological society.

Grant's Compromise

Grant takes us to the outer limits of a dependency perspective on technology. Not content to think of technique as something external to ourselves which we can examine at a distance, Grant meditates upon technology from the inside out: from the perspective of its impact on human psychology and aesthetic experience. His exhaustive exploration of the meaning of technology as dependency has been thought within the broader categories of self and civilization. In Grant's thought, two things are always at stake in any meditation on technology: the impact, both mediate and immediate, of technology on the "self"; and the implications of technological society for the broader question of the direction of western civilization. It is, perhaps, because Grant's mind oscillates between self and civilization that he is capable of offering a coherent, and internally consistent, alternative to the "darkness of the technical age". Thus, Grant counterposes the image of an "ethics of charity" to the dominance of "calculation" in the public realm; and in *Philosophy in the Mass Age*, he presents "mythic consciousness" as a precious, though perhaps futile, alternative to "instrumental activism".

But if Grant is fully radical in his understanding of the human deprivals which are the price of technological society and if he is fully courageous in thinking through the relationship between technology and the "spirit of revenge", then it must also be said that there is a deep compromise in his thought. This is a thinker who ultimately refuses to follow through on the hard implications of his philosophy. While Grant's pronouncements on history (liberalism) might be downbeat, his reassurances in favour of an absolute standard of social justice (religion) are entirely upbeat. In Grant's world, justice is never inserted into history or, for that matter, enucleated as one, highly relative aspect of the human situation. Indeed, it might even be said that Grant can achieve such a magisterial account of the disaster triumphant of modern liberalism just because he has always enjoyed the good conscience of a thinker who holds in reserve an *ahistorical* conception of justice. If it is true that it's easy today to be a conservative in Canada (complaining all the while about the quality of the ride in the back seat of the chauffered American limousine), then it's even easier to be a historical fatalist in North America. Grant wants it both ways: he condemns liberalism for its impoverishment of social justice; but he refuses to submit his faith in an absolute standard of morality (natural law) to the test of historical struggle. In the end, Grant is a Nietzschean on history, but a Christian thinker of the fatalist kind on the question of justice. Just like the technocrats and the Kantians and the liberals before him, Grant also cuts and runs before a world which yields no meaning. But unlike his liberal adversaries, Grant's will to self-preservation has this moment of nobility. Against the terrible injustices of modern times, Grant wishes to preserve an absolute and uncompromising vision of evil.

Grant once remarked, in *Philosophy in the Mass Age*, that his quest was for a "categorical limit of the wrong."[89] And he also said, in the last pages of *Time as History*, that he could not accept Nietzsche's conclusions on *amor fati*, but would have to turn back to some image of our fate "as enfolded in a timeless eternity."[90] Grant finds a "categorical limit of the wrong" in his acknowledgement of the primacy of God; and his turning back from Nietzsche's challenge to live through time as history takes him directly to privileging "remembrance" as an essential human act.

In a superb text on American thought, *The Wilderness and the City*, Michael Weinstein has said of William James that, at the moment of his discovery of the void in human experience, he developed a bad case of "panic fear."[91] James broke away from the terrible implications of his insight into the abyss in human experience; and the result was that American thought has been running ever since, from existentialism to pragmatism. In a way strikingly similar to James' compromise in his fit of "panic fear", the French thinker, Roland Barthes, remarked in *The Empire of Signs* that in the face of the radical anxiety of modern experience, he developed "panic boredom."[92] While James' "panic fear" drove his thought directly into the cheap optimism of pragmatism, Barthes' "panic boredom" condemned his meditation to a fantastically tense, almost traumatic, detachment from the vicissitudes of experience. In a way similar to James and Barthes, I would claim that Grant's thought evinces every sign of "panic remembrance." He has taken us to the very edge of Nietzsche's world; but then Grant breaks, heading directly for the sinecure of natural law. Placing his bets on remembrance of things past (historical fatalism) and on a "categorical imperative of the wrong" (abstract justice), Grant turns his back to the problem of mediating justice *and* politics in the twentieth-century. His philosophy has no means of translation into politics. Thus, the great paradox. Grant, the very thinker who has flailed the participants of the technological dynamo for living so blindly within the horizon of the will to self-preservation, short-circuits his own analysis by seeking to provide an absolute and fixed standard of justice as a consolation against the cries of the "tortured self" for meaning.

Grant is a thinker of genuine probity, but his panic remembrance marks at once the limit of his critique of technological society and the threshold that thought on technology, which wishes to surpass Grant but preserve his wealth of precious insights, shall have to overcome. Grant never promised us anything more. All of his writings are those of a tragic philosopher, the specific nobility of whose meditation derives from the fact that, long out of custom and against the dark spirit of the times, it represents an elegant and tortured recovery of the possibility of some "fundamental good" which might surpass the horror of the modern age. Grant is a romantic in the most bitter sense of the term. He is a Canadian thinker who surveys the human situation with a love which is experienced only by those who have lived and thought deeply.

> . . . that love must come out of having grasped into one's consciousness the worst that can be remembered or imagined — the torturing of children and the screams of the innocent.[93]

3

Technological Humanism:
The Processed World
of Marshall McLuhan

Popular Culture

Marshall McLuhan and George Grant represent the polarities of the Canadian mind on the question of technology. In much the same way that McLuhan in his introduction to *Empire and Communications* described Innis' staple theory of communication in terms of a grand, internal tension between "ground" and "figure"[1], we might now think of Grant as ground to McLuhan's figure. Grant is the Canadian thinker who has given the fullest and most eloquent expression to the perspective of technological dependency. But while Grant is the philosopher of the margin, McLuhan's favourite aphorism was that we now live in a society, which being electronic and thus simultaneous and integral, is "all centre without margins."[2] Grant's thought is historical in its direction, tragic in its sensibility, and a matter of remembrance. He is a witness to that which has been lost in the coming-to-be of the technological dynamo. In Grant's world, *time* is privileged as we listen for the "intimations of deprival" that might remind us of some lost human good, of precious aspects of experience, which have been cancelled by the technological imperative. But this is to say that Grant is *ground* to Canadian thought: his perspective privileges content over form, time over space. McLuhan's perspective on technology is the opposite. McLuhan is *figure* to the Canadian imagination: his perspective is all form, metaphor, and paradox. Grant may write in the fully tragic terms of a lament, but McLuhan gives us a "galaxy." To Grant's sense of historical remembrance, McLuhan counterposes the image of the "probe"[3] charting the cultural geography of the new media of communication. And to Grant's haunting image of trapped beings, "half-flesh/half-metal", McLuhan speaks of "cosmic man"[4] caught up in a more cosmopolitan, and Darwinian, struggle among competing media of communication which gain primacy as extensions of the "social and psychic faculties"[5] only as the already obsolescent content of new technological media. Grant is an *existentialist* who focusses on the image of the dominated "self" in technological society. McLuhan, however, is a *rhetorician* who privileges the aesthetic value of creative freedom as the locus of a "redeemed" human civilization.

Indeed, Grant's thought-world (fully exploring the detritus of the Protestant mind in North America) has its television analogue in CBC's epic production, *Empire,* which dwells on what the Red Tory side of the Canadian mind has always liked doing best — losing in a world in which the deck is stacked against them. And if this is so, then the television analogue of McLuhan's world is to be found in the opening sequence of CBC's, *The Journal,* which is, in any event, a perfect satire on the technological massage. In this video sequence, the camera zooms in from outer space, lingers for an instant on the geographical image of Canada, and then begins a quick global skywalk. Instantly, the geographical representation of Canada, and of the world, is transformed into perfect technocratic modules. In this beautiful and seductive, but also grisly, sequence, the camera moves from west to east only to terminate with the sun rising on a world which has been imprisoned within a technocratic image-system. Everything is de-territorialized and de-historicized: an unforgettable reminder of the incarceration of geography, and of society, within the silent medium of technology. It is a perfect image of the silent, inner workings of the technological sensorium. Indeed, this movement from the survival themes of *Empire* to the fascination with technology as a reality-effect of *The Journal* is the difference between Grant and McLuhan. McLuhan's world is that of the "technological sensorium"[7] and, consequently, of the imposition upon society of the invisible environment of new electronic technologies of communication. While Grant may have deepened and intensified our understanding of the relationship between technology and empire, McLuhan's project was to break the spell cast upon the human mind by electronic technologies — radio, television, computers, video games — which operate in the language of seduction and power. This is to say that McLuhan was a radical empiricist in his explorations of technological society. He understood immediately that technologies of communication in the electronic age overthrow the privileged position of the "contents" of the media, substituting a new sign-language of rhetorical and symbolic effects. This is the age of the enclosure of whole societies within designed environments, of metaphor, and of MEDIA. McLuhan's intention was to create anti-environments by which the silent massage of the electronic media could be revealed. He was therapist to a population mesmerized, and thus paralyzed, by the charisma of technology. While Grant ennobled the conservative side of the Canadian mind by transforming its immanent critique of technological society into an eloquent and persuasive meditation on the eclipse of modernity, McLuhan expressed that which is most insightful in the liberal side of the Canadian imagination. He sought to recover the civilizing moment in the processed world of technological society by developing a critical humanism appropriate to the popular culture of North America.

Processed World

Not the least of McLuhan's contributions to the study of technology was that he transposed the literary principle of metaphor/metonymy (the play between structure and process) into a historical methodology for analysing the rise and fall of successive media of communication. In McLuhan's discourse, novels are the already obsolescent content of television; writing "turned a spotlight on the high, dim Sierras of speech";[8] the movie is the "mechanization of movement and gesture"; the telegraph provides us with "diplomacy without walls";[10] just as "photography is the mechanization of the perspective painting and the arrested eye".[11] To read McLuhan is to enter into a "vortex" of the critical, cultural imagination, where "fixed perspective" drops off by the way, and where everything passes over instantaneously into its opposite. Even the pages of the texts in *Explorations, The Medium is the Massage, The Vanishing Point,* or *From Cliché to Archetype* are blasted apart, counterblasted actually, in an effort to make reading itself a more subversive act of the artistic imagination. Faithful to his general intellectual project of exposing the invisible environment of the technological sensorium, McLuhan sought to make of the text itself a "counter-gradient" or "probe" for forcing to the surface of consciousness the silent structural rules, the "imposed assumptions" of the technological environment within which we are both enclosed and "processed". In *The Medium is the Massage,* McLuhan insisted that we cannot understand the technological experience from the outside. We can only comprehend how the electronic age "works us over" if we "recreate the experience" in depth and mythically, of the processed world of technology.

> All media work us over completely. They are so persuasive in their personal, political, economic, aesthetic, psychological, moral, ethical, and social consequences that they leave no part of us untouched, unaffected, unaltered. The medium is the massage. Any understanding of social and cultural change is impossible without a knowledge of the way media work as environments.[12]

And McLuhan was adamant on the immanent relationship of technology and biology, on the fact that "the new media... are nature"[13] and this for the reason that technology refers to the social and psychic "extensions" or "outerings" of the human body or senses. McLuhan could be so universal and expansive in his description of the media of communication — his studies of communication technologies range from writing and speech to the telephone, photography, television, money, comic books, chairs and wrenchs — because he viewed all technology as the pushing of the "archetypal forms of the unconscious out into social consciousness."[14] When McLuhan noted in *Counter Blast* that "environment is process, not container",[15] he meant just this: the effect of all new technologies is to impose, silently and pervasively, their deep assumptions upon the human psyche by reworking the "ratio of the senses."

> All media are extensions of some human faculty — psychic or physical.[16]

> Media, by altering the environment, evoke in us unique ratios of sense perceptions. The extension of any one sense alters the way we think and act — the way we perceive the world. When these ratios change, MEN CHANGE.[17]

For McLuhan, it's a processed world now. As we enter the electronic age with its instantaneous and global movement of information, we are the first human beings to live completely within the *mediated* environment of the technostructure. The "content" of the technostructure is largely irrelevant (the "content" of a new technology is always the technique which has just been superceded: movies are the content of television; novels are the content of movies) or, in fact, a red herring distracting our attention from the essential secret of technology as the medium, or environment, within which human experience is programmed. It was McLuhan's special genius to grasp at once that the content (metonymy) of new technologies serves as a "screen", obscuring from view the disenchanted locus of the technological experience in its purely "formal" or "spatial" properties. McLuhan wished to escape the "flat earth approach" to technology, to invent a "new metaphor" by which we might "restructure our thoughts and feelings" about the subliminal, imperceptible environments of media effects.[18]

In this understanding, technology is an "extension" of biology: the expansion of the electronic media as the "metaphor" or "environment" of twentieth-century experience implies that, for the first time, the central nervous system itself has been exteriorized. It is our plight to be processed through the technological simulacrum; to participate intensively and integrally in a "technostructure" which is nothing but a vast simulation and "amplification" of the bodily senses. Indeed, McLuhan often recurred to the "narcissus theme" in classical mythology as a way of explaining our fatal fascination with technology, viewed not as "something external" but as an extension, or projection, of the sensory faculties of the human species.

> Media tend to isolate one or another sense from the others. The result is hypnosis. The other extreme is withdrawing of sensation with resulting hallucination as in dreams or DT's, etc... Any medium, by dilating sense to fill the whole field, creates the necessary conditions of hypnosis in that area. This explains why at no time has any culture been aware of the effect of its media on its overall association, not even retrospectively.[19]

All of McLuhan's writings are an attempt to break beyond the "Echo" of the narcissus myth, to show that the "technostructure" is an extension or "repetition" of ourselves. In his essay, "The Gadget Lover", McLuhan noted precisely why the Greek myth of Narcissus is of such profound relevance to understanding the technological experience.

> The youth Narcissus (narcissus means *narcosis* or numbing) mistook his own reflection in the water for another person. *This extension of himself by mirror numbed his perceptions until he became the servomechanism of his own extended or repeated image.* The nymph Echo tried to win his love with fragments of his own speech, but in vain. He was numb. He had adapted to his extension of himself and had become a closed system. Now the point of this myth is the fact that men at once become fascinated by any extension of themselves in any material other than themselves.[20]

Confronted with the hypnotic effect of the technological sensorium, McLuhan urged the use of any "probe" — humour, paradox, analogical juxtaposition, absurdity — as a way of making visible the "total field effect" of technology as medium. This is why, perhaps, McLuhan's intellectual project actually circles back on itself, and is structured directly into the design of his texts. McLuhan makes the reader a "metonymy" to his "metaphor": he transforms the act of "reading McLuhan" into dangerous participation in a radical experiment which has, as its end, the exploration of the numbing of consciousness in the technological massage. Indeed, to read McLuhan is to pass directly into the secret locus of the "medium is the massage"; to experience anew the "media" (this time the medium of writing) as a silent gradient of ground-rules.

No less critical than Grant of the human fate in technological society, McLuhan's imagination seeks a way out of our present predicament by recovering a highly ambivalent attitude towards the *objects* of technostructure. Thus, while Grant writes in William James' sense of a "block universe" of the technological dynamo, seeing only tendencies towards domination, McLuhan privileges a historically specific study of the media of communication. In an early essay (1955), "A Historical Approach to the Media", McLuhan said that if we weren't "to go on being helpless illiterates" in the new world of technology, passive victims as the "media themselves act directly toward shaping our most intimate self-consciousness", then we had to adopt the attitude of the artist.[21] "The mind of the artist is always the point of maximal sensitivity and resourcefulness in exposing altered realities in the common culture."[22] McLuhan would make of us "the artist, the sleuth, the detective" in gaining a critical perspective on the history of technology which "just as it began with writing ends with television."[23] Unlike Grant's reflections on technology which are particularistic and existential, following a downward spiral (the famous Haligonian "humbug") into pure content: pure will, pure remembrance, pure duration, McLuhan's thought remains projective, metaphorical, and emancipatory. Indeed, Grant's perspective on technology is Protestant to the core in its contemplation of the nihilism of liberal society. But if Grant's tragic inquiry finds its artistic analogue in Colville's *To Prince Edward Island,* then McLuhan's discourse is more in the artistic tradition of Georges Seurat, the French painter, and particularly in one classic portrait, *A Sunday Afternoon on the Island of La Grande Jatte.* McLuhan always accorded Seurat a privileged position as the "art fulcrum between Renaissance visual and modern tactile. The coalescing of inner and outer, subject and object."[24] McLuhan was drawn to Seurat in making painting a "light source" (a "light through situation"). Seurat did that which was most difficult and decisive: he flipped the viewer into the "vanishing point" of the painting.[25] Or as McLuhan said, and in prophetic terms, Seurat (this "precursor of TV") presented us with a searing visual image of the age of the "anxious object."[26]

Now, to be sure, the theme of anxiety runs deep through the liberal side of the Canadian mind. This is the world of Margaret Atwood's "intolerable anxiety" and of Northrop Fryes's "anxiety structure." But McLuhan is the Canadian thinker who undertook a phenomenology of anxiety, or more precisely a historically relative study of the sources of anxiety and stress in technological society. And he did so by the simple expedient of drawing us, quickly and in depth, into Seurat's startling and menacing world of the anxious, stressful objects of technology. In his book, *Through the Vanishing Point,* McLuhan said of Seurat that "by utilizing the Newtonian analysis of the fragmentation of light, he came to the technique of divisionism, whereby each dot of paint becomes the equivalent of an actual light source, a sun, as it were. This device reversed the traditional perspective by making the viewer the vanishing point."[27] The significance of Seurat's "reversal" of the rules of traditional perspective is that he abolished, once and for all, the medieval illusion that space is neutral, or what is the same, that we can somehow live "outside" the processed world of technology. With Seurat a great solitude and, paradoxically, a greater entanglement falls on modern being. "We are suddenly in the world of the "Anxious Object" which is prepared to take the audience inside the painting process itself."[28] Following C.S. Lewis in *The Discarded Image,* McLuhan noted exactly what this "flip" in

G. Seurat. *A Sunday Afternoon on the Island of La Grande Jatte*

spatial perspective meant. Rather than *looking in* according to
the traditional spatial model of medieval discourse, modern
man is suddenly *"looking out."* "Like one looking out from the
saloon entrance onto the dark Atlantic, or from the lighted
porch upon the dark and lonely moors."[29] The lesson of
Seurat is this: modernity is coeval with the age of the "anxious
object" because we live now, fully, within the designed
environment of the technological sensorium. For McLuhan,
we are like astronauts in the processed world of technology.
We now take our "environment" with us in the form of
technical "extensions" of the human body or senses. The
technostructure is both the lens through which we experience
the world, and, in fact, the "anxious object" with which
human experience has become imperceptibly, almost
subliminally, merged.[30]

Now, McLuhan often remarked that in pioneering the DEW line, Canada had also provided a working model for the artistic imagination as an "early warning system"[32] in sensing coming shifts in the technostructure. Seurat's artistic representation of the spatial reversal at work in the electronic age, a reversal which plunges us into active participation in the "field" of technological experience, was one such early warning system. It was, in fact, to counteract our "numbing" within the age of the anxious object that McLuhan's literary and artistic imagination, indeed his whole textual strategy, ran to the baroque. As an intellectual strategy, McLuhan favoured the baroque for at least two reasons: it privileged "double perspective and contrapuntal theming"; and it sought to "capture the moment of change in order to release energy dramatically."[33] There is, of course, a clear and decisive connection between McLuhan's attraction to Seurat as an artist who understood the spatial grammar of the electronic age and his fascination with the baroque as a method of literary imagination. If, indeed, we are now "looking out" from inside the technological sensorium; and if, in fact, in the merger of biology and technology which is the locus of the electronic age, "we" have become the vanishing points of technique, then a way had to be discovered for breaching the "invisible environment"[34] within which we are now enclosed. For McLuhan, the use of the baroque in each of his writings, this constant resort to paradox, double perspective, to a carnival of the literary imagination in which the pages of the texts are forced to reveal their existence also as a "medium", was also a specific strategy aimed at "recreating the experience" of technology as massage. Between Seurat (a radar for "space as process") and baroque (a "counter-gradient"): that's the artistic strategy at work in McLuhan's imagination as he confronted the subliminal, processed world of electronic technologies.

Tracking Technology I: The Catholic Legacy

There is a deep, thematic unity in all of McLuhan's writings, extending from his later studies of technology in *Understanding Media, The Medium is the Massage, The Gutenberg*

Galaxy and *Counter Blast* to his earlier, more classical, writings in *The Interior Landscape, The Vanishing Point* and also including his various essays in reviews ranging from the *Sewanee Review* to the *Teacher's College Record*. McLuhan's discourse was culturally expansive, universalist, and spatially oriented precisely because his thought expresses the Catholic side of the Canadian, and by implication, modern mind. McLuhan's Catholicism, in fact, provided him with an epistemological strategy that both gave him a privileged vantage-point on the processed world of technology and, in any event, drove him beyond literary studies to an historical exploration of technological media as the "dynamic" of modern culture. The essential aspect of McLuhan's technological humanism is that he always remained a Catholic humanist in the Thomistic tradition: one who brought to the study of technology and culture the more ancient Catholic hope that even in a world of despair (in our "descent into the maelstrom"[35] with Poe's drowning sailor) that a way out of the labyrinth could be found by bringing to fruition the "reason" or "epiphany" of technological society. McLuhan's thought often recurred to the sense that there is an immanent moment of "reason" and a possible new human order in technological society which could be captured on behalf of the preservation of "civilization."

Thus, McLuhan was a technological humanist in a special sense. He often described the modern century as the "age of anxiety"[36] because of our sudden exposure, without adequate means of understanding, to the imploded, instantaneous world of the new information order. Indeed, in *The Medium is the Massage,* he spoke of technology in highly ambivalent terms as, simultaneously, containing possibilities for emancipation and domination. For McLuhan, a *critical* humanism, one which dealt with the "central cultural tendencies."[37] of the twentieth-century, had to confront the technological experience in its role as environment, evolutionary principle, and as second nature itself.

> Environments are not passive wrappings, but active processes which work us over completely, massaging the ratio of the senses and imposing their silent assumptions. But environments are invisible. *Their ground-rules, pervasive structure, and overall patterns elude easy perception.*[38]

McLuhan's technological humanism was at the forward edge of a fundamental "paradigm shift" in human consciousness. When McLuhan spoke of electronic technology as an extension, or outering, of the central nervous system, he also meant that modern society had done a "flip". In order to perceive the "invisible ground rules" of the technological media, we have to learn to think in reverse image: to perceive the subliminal grammar of technology as metaphor, as a simulacrum or sign-system, silently and pervasively processing human existence. After all, McLuhan was serious when he described the electric light bulb (all information, no content) as a perfect model, almost a precursor, of the highly mediated world of the "information society." McLuhan's thought was structural, analogical, and metaphorical because he sought to disclose the "semiological reduction"[39] at work in the media of communication. But unlike, for example, the contemporary French thinker, Jean Baudrillard, who, influenced deeply by McLuhan, has teased out the Nietzschean side of the processed world of television, computers, and binary architecture but whose inquiry has now dissolved into fatalism, McLuhan was always more optimistic. Because McLuhan, even as he studied the "maelstrom" of high technology, never deviated from the classical Catholic project of seeking to recover the basis for a "new universal community"[40] in the culture of technology. Unlike Grant or Innis, McLuhan could never be a nationalist because his Catholicism, with its tradition of civil humanism and its faith in the immanence of "reason", committed him to the possibility of the coming of a universal world culture. In the best of the Catholic tradition, followed out by Etienne Gilson in philosophy as much as by Pierre Elliott Trudeau in politics, McLuhan sought a new "incarnation", an "epiphany", by releasing the reason in technological experience.

Indeed, in a formative essay, "Catholic Humanism", McLuhan averred that he followed Gilson in viewing Catholicism as being directly involved in the "central cultural discoveries" of the modern age. "Knowledge of the creative process in art, science, and cognition shows the way to earthly paradise, or complete madness: the abyss or the top of mount purgatory."[41] Now McLuhan's Catholicism was not a matter of traditional faith (he was a convert), but of a calculated assessment of the importance of the Catholic conception of "reason" for interpreting, and then civilizing, technological experience. Over and again in his writings, McLuhan returned to the theme that only a sharpening and refocussing of human *perception* could provide a way out of the labyrinth of the technostructure. His ideal value was that of the "creative process in art";[42] so much so in fact that McLuhan insisted that if the master struggle of the twentieth century was between reason and irrationality, then this struggle could only be won if individuals learned anew how to make of the simple act of "ordinary human perception" an opportunity for recovering the creative energies in human experience. McLuhan was a technological humanist of the blood: his conviction, repeated time and again, was that if we are to recover a new human possibility it will not be "outside" the technological experience, but must, of necessity, be "inside" the *field* of technology. What is really wagered in the struggle between the opposing tendencies towards domination and freedom in technology is that which is most personal, and intimate, to each individual: the blinding or revivification of ordinary human perception. Or, as McLuhan said in "Catholic Humanism": "... the drama of ordinary human perception seen as the poetic process is the prime analogate, the magic casement opening on the secrets of created being."[43] And, of course, for McLuhan the "poetic process" — this recovery of the method of "sympathetic reconstruction", this "recreation" of the technological experience as a "total communication", this recovery of the "rational notes of beauty, integrity, consonance, and claritas" as the actual stages of human apprehension — was the key to redeeming the technological order.[44] If only the mass media could be harmonized with the "poetic process"; if only the media of communication could be made supportive of the "creative process" in ordinary human perception: then technological society would, finally, be transformed into a wonderful opportunity for the "incarnation" of human experience. But, of course, this meant that, fully faithful to the Catholic interpretation of human experience as a working out of the (immanent) principle of natural, and then divine, reason,

McLuhan viewed technological society as an *incarnation in the making*. Unlike the secular discourse of the modern century, McLuhan saw no artifical divisions between "ordinary human perception" and the technical apparatus of the mass media or, for that matter, between biology and technology. In this discourse, the supervening value is reason; and this to such an extent that the creative process of human perception as well as the technologies of comic books, mass media, photography, music, and movies are viewed as *relative* phases in the working out of a single process of apprehension. "... The more extensive the mass medium the closer it must approximate to the character of our cognitive faculties."[45] Or, on a different note:

> As we trace the rise of successive communication channels or links, from writing to movies and TV it is borne in on us that for their exterior artifice to be effective it must partake of the character of that interior artifice by which in ordinary perception we incarnate the exterior world. Because human perception is literally incarnation. So that each of us must *poet* the world or fashion it within us as our primary and constant mode of awareness.[46]

McLuhan's *political* value may have been the creation of a universal community of humanity founded on reason, his *axiology* may have privileged the process of communication, and his *moral* dynamic may have been the "defence of civilization" from the dance of the irrational; but his ontology, the locus of his world vision, was the recovery of the "poetic process" as both a method of historical reconstruction of the mass media and a "miracle" by which technological society is to be illuminated, once again, with meaning.

> In ordinary human perception, men perform the miracle of recreating within themselves — in their interior faculties — the exterior world. This miracle is the work of the *nous poietikos* or of the agent intellect — that is the poetic or creative process. The exterior world in every instant of perception is interiorized and recreated in a new manner. Ourselves. And in this creative work that is perception and cognition, we experience immediately that dance of Being within our faculties which provides the incessant intuition of Being.[47]

The significance of the "poetic process" as the master concept of McLuhan's technological humanism is clear. It is only by creatively interiorizing (*realistically perceiving*) the "external" world of technology, by reabsorbing into the dance of the intellect mass media as extensions of the cognitive faculties of the human species, that we can recover "ourselves" anew. It is also *individual* freedom which is wagered in McLuhan's recovery of the "miracle" of ordinary human perception.

McLuhan's intellectual strategy was not, of course, a matter of quietism. Quite the contrary, the teasing out of the "epiphany" in external experience meant intense and direct participation in the "objects" composing the techno-structure. McLuhan wanted to see *from the inside* the topography of the technological media which horizon human experience. His Catholicism, with its central discovery of a "new method of study", a new way of seeing technology, fated him to be a superb student of popular culture. Indeed, McLuhan's thought could dwell on all aspects of popular culture — games, advertisements, radio, television, and detective stories — because he viewed each of these instances of technological society as somehow "magical";[48] providing new clues concerning how the technological massage alters the "ratios of the senses" and novel opportunities for improved human perception. In much the same way, but with a different purpose, McLuhan was a practitioner of Northrop Frye's "improved binoculars." Like his favourite symbolist poets, Poe, Joyce, Eliot, and Baudelaire, McLuhan always worked backwards from effects to cause. Much like the models of the detective and the artist, he wished to perfect in the method of the "suspended judgement",[49] in the *technique of discovery* itself, a new angle of vision on technological experience.

McLuhan was, in fact, a dynamic ecologist. He sought a new, internal balance among technique, imagination and nature. But his ecological sense was based on a grim sense of realism. In his view, the "electric age" is the historical period in which we are doomed to become simultaneously, the "sex of the lifeless machine world"[50] or creative participants in a great cycle which turns society back to a new "Finn cycle."[51]

McLuhan always privileged the connection between the immediacy and simultaneity of electric circuitry and "blind, all-hearing Homer."[52] This was a "humanism" which wagered itself on a desperate encounter with the "objects" of the technological order. In *Understanding Media, Counter-Blast,* and *The Medium is the Massage,* there emerges an almost cruel description of the technological sensorium as a sign-system to which the human mind is exteriorized. Electric technology, this latest sensation of the "genus sensation", implies that we are now "outered" or "ablated" into a machine-processed world of information.[53] It is the human destiny in the modern age to be programmed by an information order which operates on the basis of algorithmic and digital logic, and which, far from conscious human intervention, continues to move through the whirring of its own servomechanisms. Thus, in *Understanding Media,* McLuhan noted

> By putting our physical bodies inside our extended nervous systems by means of electric media, we set up a dynamic by which all previous technologies that are mere extensions of hands and feet and teeth and bodily controls — all such extensions of our bodies, including cities — will be translated into information systems. Electromagnetic technology requires utter human docility and quiescence of meditation *such as now befits an organism that wears its brains outside its hide and its nerves outside its skin.*[54]

And of this "semiological wash" through the techno-structure, McLuhan said simply but starkly

> Man becomes as it were the sex organ of the machine world, as the bee of the plant world, enabling it to fecundate and to evolve ever new forms. The machine-world reciprocates man's love by expediting his wishes and desires, namely by providing him with wealth.[55]

In McLuhan's effort to humanize technology through "in-depth participation" there is reopened a more ancient debate in the western mind between the tragic imagination and the calculated optimism of the rhetoricians. In his esssay, "An Ancient Quarrel in Modern America", McLuhan described himself as a "Ciceronian humanist"[56] (better, I suppose, than the early Scottish common-sense realists in Canada who labelled themselves "Caesars of the wilderness"). McLuhan was a "Ciceronian humanist" to this extent: he was, by intellectual habit, an historian of civilization and a rhetorican. McLuhan's *rhetoric* stands, for example, to Grant's tragic lament or to Innis' "marginal man" in much the same way as that earlier debate between Lucretius and Virgil. Between the rhetorician and the tragic sensibility, there is always a contest between the attitude of intellectual futility, tinged by despair, and a pragmatic will be knowledge; between resigned melancholy and melancholy resignation.

But if McLuhan brings to bear on technology the skills of a rhetorician's imagination, then he does so as a Catholic, and not Ciceronian, humanist. McLuhan's mind represents one of the best syntheses yet achieved of the Catholic legacy as this was developed in Aquinas, Joyce, and Eliot. In a largely unremarked, but decisive, article — "Joyce, Aquinas and the Poetic Process" — McLuhan was explicit that his *epistemological strategy* for the study of technology was modelled on Aquinas' method of the "respondeo dicendum"; the tracing and retracing of thought through the "cubist landscape" of the Thomistic article.[57] McLuhan said of Aquinas that in his "method of thought" we see the fully modern mind at work. In Aquinas, as later in Joyce, there is the constant use of the "labyrinth figure" as the archetype of human cognition. "Whereas the total shape of each article, with its trinal divisions into objections, respondeo, and answers to objections, is an 'S' labyrinth, this figure is really traced and retraced by the mind many times in the course of a single article."[58] Aquinas' central contribution to modern discourse was this: his "method" of study gave a new brilliance of expression to the "technique of discovery" as the locus of the modern mind.

> His 'articles' can be regarded as vivisections of the mind in act. The skill and wit with which he selects his objections constitute a cubist landscape, an ideal landscape of great intellectual extent seen from an airplane. The ideas or objects in this landscape are by their very contiguity set in a dramatic state of tension; and this dramatic tension is provided with a dramatic peripetieia in the respondeo, and with a resolution in the answers to the objections".[59]

Now, the significance of McLuhan's recovery of Aquinas' method of the "respondeo dicendum" is that this *method* is almost perfectly autobiographical of McLuhan's own strategy for the study of technological experience. Long before McLuhan in, for example, *The Medium is the Massage*, discussed the creation of a "cubist landscape" as a counter-gradient for understanding technological media or in *The Mechanical Bride* appealed for the need to sharpen "perception", he had already adopted the "Catholic method", and Joyce's adaptation of Aquinas' "article" as his main epistemological tool for "understanding media." Indeed, it was McLuhan's achievement, fully faithful to the spirit of Joyce's writings in *Ulysses, Dubliners,* and *The Portrait,* to translate the Thomistic analysis of cognition, "namely the fact of the creative process as the natural process of apprehension, arrested and retraced",[60] into a powerful intellectual procedure for grasping the inner movement in even the most prosaic objects of popular culture. "Ordinary experience is a riot of imprecision, of impressions enmeshed in preconceptions, clichés, profanities, and impercipience. But for the true artist every experience is capable of an epiphany."[61] McLuhan may have lived with the grimly pessimistic knowledge that we had become the "sex organs of the machine world", but his intellectual spirit was optimistic, and indeed, combative. In the following passage, McLuhan is speaking of Joyce in relationship to Aquinas, but he might well have been writing his intellectual notice. Like Joyce, and for the same reason, he always preferred "comic to tragic art";[62] his conclusions may have been downbeat, but his "method" was distinctly upbeat. McLuhan's very psychology was like a counter-gradient flailing against the technostructure; this in full awareness that the "technological massage" worked us over, not from outside, but from within. The "minotaurs" to be overcome in "understanding media" were also fully *interiorized* within the human mind and body.

> Any movement of appetite within the labyrinth of cognition is a "minotaur" which must be slain by the hero artist. Anything which interferes with cognition, whether concupiscence, pride, imprecision, or vagueness is a minotaur ready to devour beauty. So that Joyce not only was the first to reveal the link between the stages of

apprehension and the creative process, he was the first to understand how the drama of cognition itself was the key archetype of all human ritual myth and legend. And thus he was able to incorporate at every point in his work the body of the past in immediate relation to the slightest current of perception.[63]

McLuhan shared with Grant, and Nietzsche, a deep understanding of "technique as ourselves", of our envelopment in the historical dynamic of technological media. But he differed from them, and consequently from the 'lament' of the Protestant mind, both by subscribing to the value of "creative freedom", and by providing a precise intellectual itinerary through which the "creative process" might be generalized in human experience.

In McLuhan's terms, everything now depends on the creation of an inner harmony, a concordance of the beauty of reason, between the "imprecision of ordinary experience" and the "cognitive power in act." This is just to note, though, exactly how central McLuhan's religious sensibility (his Catholic roots) was to his interpretation of technology. It was, in the end, from Joyce and Aquinas that he took an intellectual strategy for the exploration of technological experience: the method of "suspended judgement"; the privileging of the perception of the true artist in battle with the minotaurs which block the possible epiphany in every experience; the technique of reconstruction as discovery; a singular preference for the comic over the tragic; the abandonment of narrative in favour of the "analogical juxtaposition of character, scene, and situation". Like other advocates of Catholic humanism in the twentieth-century, McLuhan was neither an impressionist nor an expressionist, but one who stood by the "method of the profoundly analogical drama of existence as it is mirrored in the cognitive power in act."[65] For McLuhan, the recovery of *reason* in technological experience was always part of a broader religious drama: what was also at stake in the contest with the minotaurs in the labyrinth of technology was individual redemption.

Tracking Technology II: Experimental Medicine

McLuhan often recurred in his writings to Poe's figure of the "drowning sailor" who, trapped in the whirlpool without a visible means of escape, studied his situation with "calm detachment" in order to discover some thread which might lead out of the labyrinth.[66] While the Catholic touch in McLuhan's thought provided him with the necessary sense of critical detachment and, moreover, with the transcendent value of creative freedom; it was the particular genius of his discourse that he managed to combine an intellectual sensibility which was essentially Thomistic with the more ancient practice of exploring the crisis of technological society within the terms of experimental medicine. In McLuhan's inquiry, there is rehearsed time and again a classically medical approach to understanding technology: an approach which, while it may be traced directly to Hippocrates' *Ancient Medicine,* also has its origins in Thucydides' method of historical writing. Very much in the tradition of Hippocrates, and then Thucydides, McLuhan's historical study of the media of communication was structured by the three moments of semiology (classification of symptoms), diagnosis and therapeutics.[67] Indeed, it might even be said that McLuhan's adoption of the three stages of the Thomistic "article" — objections, respondeo, and answers to objections — was only a modern variation of the more classical method of experimental medicine. In both instances, the historical experience under interrogation is "recreated in depth", with special emphasis placed on the historian (the *cultural* historian as doctor to a sick society) as a "vivisectionist" of the whole field of experience.[68] When McLuhan recommended repeatedly that the cultural historian "trace and retrace" the field of technological experience, both as a means of understanding the "closure" effected upon human perspective and as a way of discovering an escape-hatch, he was only restating, in distinctly modern language, the experimental method of ancient medicine. McLuhan's imagination always played at the interface of biology and technology. His discourse took as its working premise that the most insidious effect of technology lay in its deep colonization of biology, of the body itself; and, moreover, in its implicit claim, that technology is the new locus of the evolutionary principle. For McLuhan the technological "sensorium" was precisely that: an artificial amplification, and transferral, of human consciousness and sensory organs to the technical apparatus, which now, having achieved the electronic phase of "simultaneity" and "instantaneous scope", returns to take its due on the human body.[69]. The "sensorium" presents itself to a humanity which has already passed over into "deep shock" over the inexplicable consequences of electronics as a practical *simulation* of evolution, of the biological process itself. This circling back of the technological sensorium, this silent merger of technology and biology, is the cataclysmic change in human history that so disturbed McLuhan. His discourse on technology begins and ends with an exploration of the "possession" of biology by the technological imperative. Indeed, in McLuhan's estimation, technology works its effects upon biology much like a disease. It is also the tools of a doctor which are needed both for an accurate diagnosis of the causes of the disease, and for a prognosis of some cure which might be recuperative of the human sensibility in technological society.

One pervasive theme running through McLuhan's writings has to do with the double-effect of the technological experience in "wounding" the human persona by effecting a "closure" of human perception, and in "numbing" and thus "neutralizing" the area under stress.[70] It was McLuhan's melancholy observation that when confronted with new technologies, the population passes through, and this repeatedly, the normal cycle of shock: "alarm" at the disturbances occasioned by the introduction, often on a massive scale, of new extensions of the sensory organs; "resistance" which is typically directed at the "content" of new technological innovations (McLuhan's point was, of course, that the content of a new technology is only the already passé history of a superceded technology); and "exhaustion" in the face of our inability to understand the subliminal (formal) consequences of fundamental changes in the technostructure.[71] It was his dour conclusion that, when confronted with the "paradigm-shift" typified by the transformation of technology from a mechanical, industrial model to an electronic one, the population rapidly enters into a permanent state of exhaustion and bewilderment. In McLuhan's terms, the present century is characterized by an almost total unconsciousness of the real effects of the technological media. "The new media are blowing a lot of baby powder around the pendant cradle of the NEW MAN today. The dust gets in our eyes."[72]

It was a source of great anxiety to McLuhan that electronic technologies, with their abrupt reversal of the structural laws of social and non-social evolution, had (*without* human consent or even social awareness) precipitated a new, almost autonomous, technical imperative in human experience. In *Counter Blast,* McLuhan had this to say of the new technological imperative.

> Throughout previous evolution, we have protected the central nervous system by outering this or that physical organ in tools, housing, clothing, cities. But each outering of individual organs was also an acceleration and intensification of the general environment until the central nervous system did a flip. We turned turtle. The shell went inside, the organs outside. Turtles with soft shells become vicious. That's our present state.[74]

A society of "vicious turtles" is also one in which technology works its "biological effects" in the language of stress. For McLuhan, the advent of electronic technology creates a collective sense of deep distress, precisely because this "outering" of the central nervous system induces an unprecedented level of stress on the individual organism. The "technological massage" reworks human biology and the social psyche at a deep, subliminal level. Having grasped the essential connection between technology and stress, it was not surprising that so much of McLuhan's discourse on technology was influenced by Hans Selye's pioneering work in the field of stress. Indeed, McLuhan adopted directly from Selye's research a *medical* understanding of the relationship between stress and numbness. A central theme in McLuhan's reflection on bio-technology was Selye's original theorisation that under conditions of deep stress, the organism anesthetizes the area effected, making the shock felt in peripheral regions. And McLuhan always insisted that the age of electric circuity is a time of HIGH STRESS.

> When an organ goes out (ablation) it goes numb. The central nervous system has gone numb (for survival). We enter the age of the unconscious with electronics, and consciousness shifts to the physical organs, even in the body politic. There is a great stepping up of physical awareness and a big drop in mental awareness when the central nervous system goes outward.[75]

Or again, and this in *Counter Blast*, although the same theme is also at the very beginning of *Understanding Media*:

> The one area which is numb and unconscious is the area which receives the impact. Thus there is an exact parallel with ablation in experimental medicine, but in medical ablation, observation is properly directed, not to the numb area, but to all the other organs as they are affected by the numbing or ablation of the single organ.[76]

It was McLuhan's overall project (his *semiology*) to probe the numbing of human perception by the technological innovations of the electronic age. In much the same way that McLuhan said of the movement from speech to writing that it illuminated the "high, dim Sierras of speech", McLuhan's "medical" understanding of technology lit up the darkness surrounding the invisible environment of the forms (rhetoric) of technology. All of McLuhan's writings are, in fact, a highly original effort at casting iron filings across the invisible "field" of electronic technologies in an effort to highlight their tacit assumptions. McLuhan's intention was to break the seduction-effect of technology, to disturb the hypnotic spell cast by the dynamism of the technological imperative. And thus, while he was in the habit of saying, about the "inclusive" circuitry of the electronic age, that it was composed of "code, language, mechanical medium — all (having) magical properties which transform, transfigure,"[77] he was also accustomed to note that, on the down-side of the "new age", its participants were daily "x-rayed by television images."[78]

McLuhan could be so ambivalent on the legacy of the technological experience because, following Hans Selye and Adolphe Jonas, he viewed technological media as *simultaneously* extensions *and* auto-amputations of the sensory organs. The paradoxical character of technological media as both amplifications and cancellations was, of course, one basic theme of *Understanding Media*.

> While it was no part of the intention of Jonas and Selye to provide an explanation of human invention and technology, they have given us a theory of disease (discomfort) that goes far to explain why man is impelled to extend various parts of his body by a kind of auto-amputation.[79]

It was McLuhan's special insight though, to recognize the deep relationship between the history of technological innovation and the theory of disease. McLuhan's historical account of the evolution of technological media was structured around a (medical) account of technological innovation as "counter-irritants" to the "stress of acceleration of pace and increase of load."[80] Just as the body (in Hans Selye's terms) resorts to an auto-amputative strategy when "the perceptual power cannot locate or avoid the cause of irritation", so too (in McLuhan's terms) in the stress of super-stimulation, "the central nervous system acts to protect itself by a strategy of amputation or isolation of the offending organ, sense, or function."[81] Technology is a "counter-irritant" which aids in the "equilibrium of the physical organs which protect the central nervous system."[82] Thus, the wheel (as an extension of the foot) is a counter-irritant against the sudden pressure of "new burdens resulting from the acceleration of exchange by written and monetary media"; "movies and TV complete the cycle of mechanization of the human sensorium"; and computers are ablations or outerings of the human brain itself.[83] Now, it was McLuhan's thesis that the motive-force for technological innovation was always defensive and biological: the protection of the central nervous system against sudden changes in the "stimulus" of the external environment. Indeed, McLuhan often noted that "the function of the body" was the maintenance of an equilibrium among the media of our sensory organs. And consequently, the electronic age is all the more dangerous, and, in fact, suicidal when "in a desperate... autoamputation, as if the central nervous system could no longer depend on the physical organs to be protective buffers against the slings and arrows of outrageous mechanism",[84] the central nervous system itself is outered in the form of electric circuitry. McLuhan inquires, again and again, what is to be the human fate now that with the "extension of consciousness" we have put "one's nerves outside, and one's physical organs inside the nervous system, or brain."[85] For McLuhan, the modern century is typified by an information order which plays our nerves in public: a situation, in his estimation, of "dread".

It was in an equally desperate gamble at increasing popular awareness of the "flip" done to us by the age of electric circuitry that McLuhan undertook an essentially medical survey of technological society. McLuhan's "classification of symptoms" took the form of an elaborate and historical description of the evolution of technology from the "mechanical" extensions of man (wheels, tools, printing) to the mythic, inclusive technologies of the electric age (television, movies, computers, telephone, phonograph). His "diagnosis" was that the crisis induced by technological society had much to do with the "closures" (numbing) effected among the sense ratios by new technical inventions. McLuhan was explicit about the technological origins of the modern stress syndrome: "the outering or extension of our bodies and senses in a new invention compels the whole of our bodies and senses to shift into new positions in order to maintain equilibrium."[86] A new "closure" is occasioned in our sensory organs and faculties, both private and public, by new technical extension of man. And McLuhan's "therapeutic": the deployment of the "creative imagination" as a new way of seeing technology, and of responding, mythically and in depth, to the challenges of the age of electric circuitry. For McLuhan, the stress syndrome associated with the coming-to-be of the technostructure could only be met with the assistance of educated perspective. If it is the human fate to live within its (own) central nervous system in the form of the electronic simulation of consciousness, then it is also the human challenge to respond *creatively* to the "dread" and "anxiety" of the modern age. We may be the servo-mechanisms, the body bits, of a technical apparatus which substitutes a language of codes, of processed information, for "natural" experience, but this is a human experience which is double-edged. Without the education of perspective or, for that matter, in the absence of a "multidimensional perpective"[87] on technique, it will surely be the human destiny to be imprinted by the structural imperatives, the silent grammar, of the new world information order. But it was also McLuhan's hope, occasioned by his faith in the universality of reason that the electronic age could be transformed in the direction of creative freedom. After all, it was his over-arching thesis that the era of electric circuitry represented a great break-point in human experience: the end of "visual, uniform culture"[88] based on mechanical technologies, and the ushering in of a popular culture of the "new man'. which would be fully tribal and organic. In all his texts, but particularly in *The Medium is the Massage,* McLuhan insisted on teasing out the emancipatory tendencies in new technologies. Against the blandishments of an "official culture" to impose old meanings on novel technologies, McLuhan sympathized with "anti-social perspectives": the creative perspectives of the artist, the poet, and even the young, who respond with "untaught delight to the poetry, and the beauty of the new technological environment."[89] In his intellectual commitment to the development of a new perspective on technology, McLuhan was, of course, only following Joyce in his willingness to respond to the technological environment with a sense of its "creative process." "He (Joyce) saw that the wake of human progress can disappear again into the night of sacral or auditory man. The Finn cycle of tribal institutions can return in the electric age, but if again, then let's make it a wake or awake or both".[90] Anyway in McLuhan's world, in a society which has sound as its environment, we have no choice. "We simply are not equipped with earlids."[91]

McLuhan's Blindspots

McLuhan was the last and best exponent of the liberal imagination in Canadian letters. His thought brings to a new threshold of intellectual expression the fascination with the question of technology which has always, both in political and private practice, so intrigued liberal discourse in Canada. McLuhan's thought provides a new eloquence, and indeed, nobility of meaning to "creative freedom" as a worthwhile public value; and this as much as it reasserts the importance of a renewed sense of "individualism", both as the locus of a revived political community and as a creative site (the "agent intellect") for releasing, again and again, the possible "epiphanies" in technological experience. In McLuhan's writings, the traditional liberal faith in the *reason* of technological experience, a reason which could be the basis of a rational and universal political community, was all the more ennobled to the extent that the search for the "reason" in technology was combined with the Catholic quest for a new "incarnation." McLuhan's communication theory was a direct outgrowth of his Catholicism; and his religious sensibility fused perfectly with a classically liberal perspective on the question of technology and civilization. In the present orthodoxy of intellectual discourse, it is not customary to find a thinker whose inquiry is both infused by a transcendent religious sensibility and whose intellectual scholarship is motivated, not only by a desperate sense of the eclipse of reason in modern society, but by the disappearance of "civilization" itself through its own vanishing-point. As quixotic as it might be, McLuhan's intellectual project was of such an inclusive and all-embracing nature. His thought could be liberal, Catholic, and structuralist (before his time) precisely because the gravitation-point of McLuhan's thought was the preservation of the fullest degree possible of creative freedom in a modern century, which, due to the stress induced by its technology, was under a constant state of emergency. In McLuhan's discourse, individual freedom as well as civil culture itself were wagered in the contest with technology. The technological experience also made the possibility of a new "incarnation" fully ambivalent: it was also the Catholic, and by extension, liberal belief in a progressive, rational, and evolutionary history which was gambled in the discourse on technology.

But if McLuhan provides an important key to exploring the technological media, then it must also be noted that there are, at least, two major limitations in his thought which reduce his value, either as a guide to understanding technology in the Canadian circumstance or, for that matter, to a full inquiry into the meaning of the technological experience in the New World. First, McLuhan had no systematic, or even eclectic, theory of the relationship between economy and technology; and certainly no critical appreciation of the appropriation, and thus privatisation, of technology by the lead institutions, multinational corporations and the state, in advanced industrial societies. It was not, of course, that McLuhan was unaware of the relationship of corporate power and technology. One searing sub-text of *Understanding Media* and *The Mechanical Bride* had to do with the almost malignant significance of the corporate control of electronic technologies. In McLuhan's estimation, "technology is part of our bodies.';[92] and to the extent that corporations acquire private control over the electronic media then we have, in effect, "leased out" our eyes, ears, fingers, legs, and the brain itself, to an exterior power.[93] In the electronic age, this era of collective and integral consciousness, those with control of technological media are allowed "to play the strings of our nerves in public."[94] The body is fully externalized, and exposed, in the interstices of the technological sensorium. For McLuhan, just like Grant, the technological dynamo breeds a new formation of power, demonic and mythic, which is capable, as one of its reflexes of vapourizing the individual subject, and of undermining all "public" communities. But if McLuhan understood the full dangers of corporate control of technological media, nowhere did he extend this insight into a reflection on the relationship of capitalism and technology. Now, it may be, as in the case of Jacques Ellul, another civil humanist, that McLuhan's intellectual preference was to privilege the question of technology over all other aspects of social experience, including the economic foundations of society. McLuhan may have been a technological determinist, or at the minimum, a "technological monist" who took *technique* to be the primary locus for the interpretation of society as a whole. If this was so, then it is particularly unfortunate since McLuhan's "blindspot" on the question of capitalism and technology undermined, in the end, his own injunction for an "historical understanding" of the evolution of technological media. In "Catholic Humanism" and, for that matter, in all of his writings, McLuhan urged the use of the historical imagination — an historical perspective which was to be sympathetic, realistic, and reconstructive — as our only way of understanding the great watershed in human experience precipitated by the appearance of electronic society. His was, however, a curious and somewhat constricted vision of the historical imagination: for it omitted any analysis of the precise historical conditions surrounding the development of the technological experience in North America. McLuhan was as insensitive, and indifferent, to the problem of the political economy of technology as he was to the relationship of technology and ideological hegemony in the creation of liberal society, and the liberal state, in North America. McLuhan's primary value was, of course, creative freedom, not "justice"; and his political preference was for a universal community founded on the rights of "reason", not for the "ethic of charity." This is to say, however, that McLuhan's "historical sense" already embraced, from its very beginnings, the deepest assumptions of technological society. McLuhan's mind was a magisterial account of the technological imagination itself. This was a discourse which evinced a fatal fascination with the utopian possibilities of technology. Indeed, McLuhan liked to speculate about the almost religious utopia immanent in the age of information.

> Language as the technology of human extension, whose powers of division and separation we know so well, may have been the "Tower of Babel" by which men sought to scale the highest heavens. Today computers hold out the promise of a means of instant translation of any code or language into any other code or language. The computer, in short, promises by technology a Pentecostal condition of universal understanding and unity. The next logical step

would seem to be, not to translate, but to by-pass languages in favour of a general cosmic consciousness which might be very like the collective unconscious dreamt by Bergson. The condition of "weightlessness" that biologists say promises a physical immortality, may be paralleled by the condition of speechlessness that could confer a perpetuity of collective harmony and peace.[95]

Everything in McLuhan's thought strained towards the liberation of the "Pentecostal condition" of technology: the privileging of space over time; the fascination with the exteriorisation in electronic technology of an "inner experience" which is electric, mythic, inclusive, and configurational; the primacy of "field" over event; the vision of "processed information" as somehow consonant with the perfectibility of the human faculties. And it was this utopian, and transcendent, strain in McLuhan's thought which may, perhaps, have made it impossible for his inquiry to embrace the problematic of capitalism and technology. In McLuhan's lexicon, the privileging of the "economic" relationship belonged to an obsolete era: the now superceded age of specialism, fragmentation, and segmentation of work of the industrial revolution. McLuhan viewed himself as living on the other side, the far side, of technological history: the coming age of "cosmic man" typified by "mythic or iconic awareness" and by the substitution of the "multi-faceted for the point-of-view."[96] What was capitalism? It was the obsolescent content of the new era of the electronic simulation of consciousness. For McLuhan, economy had also gone electronic and thus even the corporate world, with its "magic" of advertisements and its plenitude of computers, could be subsumed into the more general project of surfacing the reason in technological society. Consequently, it might be said that McLuhan's blindspot on the question of economy was due not so much to a strain of "technological determinism" in his thought, and least not in the *first* instance; but due rather to his, transparently Catholic expectation that if the electronic economy of the corporate world was not an "agent intellect" in the creation of a new technological horizon, it was, at least, a necessary catalyst in setting the conditions for "cosmic man." McLuhan was a "missionary" to the power centres of the technological experience; and he could so faithfully, and guilelessly, discuss the civilizing moment in technology because there never was any incompatibility between the Catholic foundations of his communication theory and the will to empire. If McLuhan was a deeply compromised thinker, then it was because his Catholic humanism allowed him to subordinate, and forget, the question of the private appropriation of technology. And what was, in the final instance, tragic and not comic about his intellectual fate was simply this: it was precisely the control over the speed, dissemination, and implanting of new technologies by the corporate command centres of North America which would subvert the very possibility of an age of "creative freedom".

If one limitation in McLuhan's discourse on technology was his forgetfulness of the mediation of technology by political economy, then a second limitation, or arrest, concerned McLuhan's contempt for the "national question" in Canada. It would be unfair to criticize a thinker for not violating the internal unity of his own viewpoint. McLuhan was always firm in his belief that the dawn of the "global village", this new era of "universal understanding and unity" required the by-passing of "national" political communities. The universalism of reason and the potentically new "Finn cycle" of an all-inclusive and mythic technological experience rendered obsolete *particularistic* political concerns. McLuhan's polis was the world; and his, not inaccurate, understanding of that world had it that the United States, by virtue of its leadership in electronic technologies, was the "new world environment."[97] It was, consequently, with a noble conscience that McLuhan, like Galbraith, Easton, and Johnson before him, could turn his attention southward, passing easily and with no sign of disaffection, into the intellectual centres of the American empire. And, of course, in prophesying the end of nationalist sensibility, or the more regional sense of a "love of one's own", McLuhan was only following the flight beyond "romanticism" of the liberal political leadership of Canada, and, in particular, the "creative leadership" of Trudeau. Indeed, that Trudeau could so instantly and enthusiastically embrace McLuhan's world-sensibility was only because the latter's sense of an underlying reason in the technological order confirmed the deepest prejudices of Trudeau's own political perspective. Indeed, between Trudeau and McLuhan a parallel project was in the making: on Trudeau's part (*Federalism and the French-Canadians*) a political challenge against the "obsolete" world of ethnicity (and thus nationalism) in Québec and an invitation to Québec to join the technological (rational) society of North America; and on McLuhan's part, an epistemological and then moral decision to join in the feast of corporate advantages spread out by the masters of the empire. The common trajectories traced by Trudeau's technocratic politics and by McLuhan's sense of technological utopia reveals, powerfully so, the importance of the Catholic touch in Canadian politics and letters; just as much as it reflects, that for the empire at least, Catholicism is, indeed, intimate with the "central cultural discoveries" of the modern age. Moreover, the very existence of a "McLuhan" or a "Trudeau" as the locus of the Canadian discourse discloses the indelible character of Canada, not just as a witness to empire, but, perhaps, as a radical experiment in the working out of the intellectual and political basis of the technological imagination in North America. Canada is, and has always been, the most modern of the New World societies; because the character of its colonialism, of its domination of the land by technologies of communication, and of its imposition of an "abstract nation" upon a divergent population by a fully technological polity, has made of it a leading expression of technological liberalism in North America.

It was, consequently, the fate of McLuhan to be welcomed into the privileged circles of the corporate and intellectual elites of the United States. This was not unanticipated. The Canadian philosopher, Charles Norris Cochrane, noted that it is the peculiar feature of imperialisms that, as their energies focus, in the most mature phase of empire, on the "pragmatic will" to conquer, to expand, to live, they are often forced to seek out in the peripheral regions of the empire some new source of intellectual energy, some inspiring historical justification, which would counter the dawning sense of "intellectual futility" that so often accompanies, and undermines, the greatest successes of the will to empire.[98] McLuhan was such an "historical energizer." His utopian vision of technological society provided the corporate leadership of the American empire with a sense of historical destiny; and, at least, with the passing illusion that their narrow-minded concentration on the "business" of technology might make of them the "Atlas" of the new world of cosmic man. It was McLuhan's special ability, done, no doubt, sometimes tongue in cheek and with a proper sense of intellectual cynicism, to transfigure the grubby leadership (Grant's "creative leaders") of the American business world, and then of a good part of the new class of technocrats in the West, into the dizzying heights of a greater historical destiny, that made him such a favoured courtesan of the technological empire. Grant might say of the "creative leaders" of empire that their nihilism is such that they would always prefer to will rather than not to will, but McLuhan provided another, more radical, alternative. In the face of the incipient nihilism of the technological experience, McLuhan dangled that most precious of gifts: a sense of historical purpose (the age of communications as "cosmic consciousness"); and an intellectual justification (the technological imperative as both necessary *and* good).

While Grant's austere, and forbidding, description of technological dependency revolved around a consideration of *technique as will,* McLuhan thought of technique as possessing, at least potentially, the *poetry of consciousness.* Thus, it was not with bad faith but with the curious amorality of a thinker whose ethic, being as it was abstract freedom and reason, and who could thus screen out the barbarism of the technological dynamo, that McLuhan could associate with the leadership of technological society. And just to the extent that Grant's ruminations on technological society have led him into, almost self-imposed, solitude in Halifax (far from the "dynamic centre" of the technological dynamo in the Great Lakes region of North America), McLuhan could be a dandy of the New York intelligentsia. McLuhan's association of the values of reason and "universal unity" with the expansive momentum of the technostructure was, of course, a highly fortuitous compromise. It allowed him to serve a legitimation function for the technological dynamo, while all the while maintaining his *sang-froid* as a civil humanist who was above the fray, a Catholic intellectual among the barbarians.

McLuhan's political commitments, represented both by his rejection of the "national question" in Canada and by his participation, in depth, in the futurology of technological empire, are of direct consequence to his contributions to a master theory of communications. That McLuhan could find no moment of deviation between his civil humanism, founded on the defence of "civilization", and his absorption into the intellectual appendages of empire, indicates, starkly and dramatically, precisely how inert and uncritical is the supervening value of "civilization". McLuhan's lasting legacy is, perhaps, a historical one: the inherent contradiction of his discourse in remaining committed to the very techno-structure which had destroyed the possibility of "civilization" indicates the ultimate failure of civil humanism in modern politics. McLuhan's humanism, and indeed his abiding Catholicism, could provide an inspiring vision of a more utopian human future; but in remaining tied to the "primacy of reason", a *reason* which was fully abstracted from history and ontology, McLuhan's discourse could always be easily turned from within. This was the comic aspect of the whole affair: the technological dynamo could also accept as its dominant value the "primacy of reason"; and, by extension, the application of technical reason, in politics, bureaucracy, science, and industry, to the proliferation of technological media. The technostructure thus absorbed McLuhan's discourse on his own terms: it transposed his search for a new, universal civilization into an historical justification of technological necessitarianism; and it showed precisely how compatible the Catholic conception of "transcendent reason" is with the rationalising impulses of the technological system. McLuhan's one possible avenue of escape: the recovery of a "grounded" and emergent cultural practice or, at least, some sense of "intimations of deprival" which had been silenced by the technological dynamo was, of course, firmly closed to him by his commitment to the universal over the local, and to the metaphorical over the historical. To dismiss McLuhan as a technological determinist is to miss entirely the point of his intellectual contribution. McLuhan's value as a theorist of culture and technology began just when he went over the hill to the side of the alien and surrealistic world of mass communications: the "real world" of technology where the nervous system is exteriorised and everyone is videoated daily like sitting screens for television. Just because McLuhan sought *to see* the real world of technology, and even to celebrate technological reason as freedom, he could provide such superb, first-hand accounts of the new society of electronic technologies. McLuhan was fated to be trapped in the deterministic world of technology, indeed to become one of the intellectual servomechanisms of the machine-world, because his Catholicism failed to provide him with an adequate cultural theory by which to escape the hegemony of the abstract media systems that he had sought to explore. Paradoxically, however, it was just when McLuhan became most cynical and most deterministic, when he became fully aware of the nightmarish quality of the "medium as massage", that his thought becomes most important as an entirely creative account of the great paradigm-shift now going on in twentieth-century experience. McLuhan was then, in the end, trapped in the "figure" of his own making. His discourse could provide a brilliant understanding of the inner fuctioning of the technological media; but no illumination concerning how "creative freedom" might be won through in the "age of anxiety, and dread." In a fully tragic sense, McLuhan's final legacy was this: he was the playful perpetrator, and then victim, of a sign-crime.[99]

4

Technological Realism:
Harold Innis' Empire
of Communications

The Historical Imagination

There is a brilliant, and haunting, production by the prairie artist, Don Proch, which is fully suggestive of the contribution of Harold Innis to an understanding of the technological experience. Titled *Manitoba Mining Mask*, the work is in the form of a sculpture of the human head. The exterior of the mask is a careful, and detailed, representation of an industrial landscape, a mining site, which is imposed on the natural landscape. Immediately, we are presented with a scene of devastation; if not indeed, with a summational vision of the meaning of the colonization of the landscape by modern technology. Everywhere there is an almost funereal

Don Proch. *Manitoba Mining Mask*

sense of the victory of the power of death, and immobility, over life. Fumes from the mining site are reproduced in the form of bleached chicken bones; the forest is carved out at will in a perfect representation of the meeting of technique and the land; and, as Kenneth Hughes, a contemporary Manitoba writer, has said of this work: "Even the mining shafts are in the form of dead eyes".[1]

Now, all of Proch's artistic productions, ranging from *Manitoba Mining Mask* to *Chicken Bone Mask*, *Prairie Plough Mask*, and *Night Landing* offer a starkly realistic, and grisly, image of the overwhelming effect of technocracy in reworking the landscapes of nature and of the human imagination. And, to the extent that Proch presents technology as an active and inclusive social process, involving specific techniques as well as its own rationality, values, and economic principles, the use of the mask signifies that we are locked within the technological experience. Again, following the analysis of Hughes, what appears on the outside of the mask signifies what the person sees from the inside. In *Manitoba Mining Mask*,

we are as close as possible to what the Canadian anthro-
pologist, Edmund Carpenter, warned would be the human
fate when confronted with the power of technology: "They
became what they beheld."[2] *Manitoba Mining Mask* is,
consequently, an eloquent depiction of the fusion of
biography and history, of agency and structure, in
technological experience. Proch's masks visually represent
the impact of industrial technology massaging the human
brain, and suppressing both organic matter and human vision.
They are almost *suffocating* images of life in contemporary
society; and Proch implies that technological experience,
understood as a complex and multidimensional social
process, also traps us in its own way of seeing, and
interpreting, machine culture. Proch thus provides a deep,
psychological insight into the functioning of the technical
system. It is our fate as inhabitants of the modern world to live
in the midst of a megatension between technology and
geography, between our existence as historical beings and the
technological apparatus which entraps us.

Writing in *Saturday Night*, Adele Freeman heads an article
with the words "Don Proch is the shaman of prairie art":[3] the
mask has a symbolic, mythological meaning. This shamanistic
quality of the mask has been described eloquently by Karyn
Allen in her review of Proch's contribution to an important
exhibit: *The Winnipeg Pespective 1981 — Ritual*.

> The donning of the mask as a means of summoning an
> absent spirit is a central practice of shamanistic rites. The
> ritual implication is that, by the wearing of the mask, one
> exchanges identities with the spirit implied by the mask's
> symbols and images. In several of Proch's own masks there
> is an implied interchange, or fusion, between the human
> and imagistic elements. In other of his masks, the
> shamanistic notion of the mask as protection from the evil
> spirits might be inferred. The *Manitoba Mining Mask* is an
> obvious example.[4]

If Proch can correctly be described as "the shaman of
prairie art", it is because in the donning of the mask he seeks
to make us fully aware of the bias of technology, both in
transforming, and "screening off", the environment,

imprisoning us within the seductive vision of the technological imagination. Proch's therapeutic against our
investiture by the technical system is also clear. Only by
putting on the mask of technology, by, that is, absorbing fully
the technological experience as a dynamic social process
within which we are implicated as historical beings, can we
hope to begin the long and delicate process of healing, first a
damaged human sensibility and, then, a damaged natural
environment. As in *Manitoba Mining Mask*, Proch's artistic
imagination exists at that threshold where the hell of
technical dependency passes over into its opposite: the new
morning of an emancipated human history.

Like Proch, but this time at the level of the *historical*
imagination, Harold Innis is the shaman of the Canadian
discourse on technology. Each of Innis' major writings, from
The Cod Fisheries, *The Fur Trade in Canada*, *A History of the
Canadian Pacific Railway* to *The Bias of Communication*, *Empire and
Communications* and *The Strategy of Culture*, represent, in a fully
participatory fashion, the "donning of the mask" of technology. It was Innis' particular genius to make us see *from
within* the bias of technology, both as the locus of Canadian
economic history and as the "horizon" surrounding the
working-out of the Canadian fate in a turbulent world. And
just like the great quality of "truthfulness" which is central to
the appeal of *Manitoba Mining Mask*, Innis' work is without
illusions and without a commitment to hypocrisy. Innis once
said, with an unrelenting sense of the marginality of the
intellectual in machine culture, that it is "...not only
dangerous in this country to be a social scientist with an
interest in truth but it is exhausting."[5] As a methodological,
but also moral, practice, Innis always insisted that it was only
by reliving in depth the actual history of industrial technology —
its economy, politics, psychology, and culture — that we
could achieve a thorough understanding of the political
economy of modern technology or, what was more significant,
the relationship between technology and civilization in North
America. And faithful to his word, reading Innis takes us into
the deepest interstices of the technological experience,
understood as the primal of Canadian society. In Innis' writings,
it is the historical imagination *par excellence* which pours over,

dissects, and reconstructs the story of industrial technology in its application, first to the Canadian discourse and, by way of thematic extension, to western civilization as a whole. Everything is there: an *economic* examination of the relationship among feudalism, commercialism, and industrialism as three moments in the deeply entangled history of capitalism and technology in the Canadian setting; a *psychological* analysis of the character-type — the "aggressive individualism" of the central Canadian elite — which fueled the expansionary momentum of technique across the wilderness; a *political* diagnosis of the relationship between the "staples economy" and Canadian politics ("Canada emerged as a political entity with boundaries largely determined by the fur trade," *The Fur Trade in Canada*); and a *cultural* analysis of the sources of the deep colonialism of the Canadian mind (a combination of a "counter-revolutionary tradition" and "puritanical smugness").[6] In Innis' use of the historical imagination, we are swept away into a richly textured discourse on technology, which while it may begin with an elegant, and almost *biological*, series of case studies of "staples commodities" (cod, fur, lumber, pulp and paper, wheat, etc.,) in the Canadian past quickly explodes outwards into an entirely original, and important, meditation on the estrangement of time and space as the degree-zero of the crisis of western civilization. Indeed, Innis could be simultaneously a poet, economist, philosopher, and cultural theorist because he never forgot that the main task of the historical imagination was to provide its participants with *mediations* between biography and history. Almost as if his writings were running alongside and in full sympathy with the radical critique of the American thinker, C. Wright Mills (*The Sociological Imagination*), Innis was determined to create a fusion-point between our individual circumstance as historical beings buffeted by social forces beyond our control and the silent language of industrial technology which structures social experience. Thus, Innis draws us deep inside the vortices of the technological experience; and he does so by creating nothing less than a phenomenology of modern experience. To read Innis is to become aware, intensely and immediately, of our conditioning by the social process of modern technology: a social process which thematizes reason ("machine rationality"), will ("utility as the modern nullity"), feeling ("present mindedness"), and organization ("spatially biased media of communication").[7] Innis' insistence on "truth-seeking" yields an entirely austere and bitter lesson. It is our fate as Canadians to be formed by a history of technological dependency (Innis is clear: Canada is the reflex of the dynamic will to mastery of three empires — French, British, and American);[8] and to be pulled from ahead by a modern "civilization" which finds "its own method of suicide" in the radical division of time and space.[9] It is only one, but certain, sign of Innis' willingness to "don the mask" of technology, that he returned often in his writings to that seminal political reflection in Herodotus: "The ultimate bitterness is this: to have consciousness of much; but control over nothing."[10]

But if Innis' creative, and exhaustive, use of the historical imagination shows us precisely how, when, where and why Canadian being is a reflex of the discourse on technology, of the fateful encounter of technique and geography, then it also contains an emancipatory vision. Innis concluded his master essay, "A Plea for Time", with the biblical injunction: "Without vision the people perish."[11] In a certain sense, all of his writings, from the early naturalistic studies of the "disasters which overtook North American civilization with the coming of the Europeans"[12] to his later philosophical reflections on the "fanaticism" of American empire,[13] were an attempt to recover the spirit of the land, and of its people, which had been silenced by industrial development. Indeed, to the extent that Innis' most mature writings, *The Bias of Communication* and *Empire and Communications*, had as their central thesis that in "Western civilization a stable society is dependent on an appreciation of a proper balance between the concepts of space (territory) and time (duration)",[14] then all of Innis' writings might be interpreted as a recovery of time, of historical remembrance, against the "monopolies of space" (radio, television, newspapers — the detritus of "machine culture") imposed by technological society.[15] Almost in the speculative and experimental tradition of the best of science fiction, in the tradition, for example, of Stephen Delany's *Triton* or Ursula K. Le Guin's *The Left Hand of Darkness*, Innis' historical imagination takes the form of a time-traveller in the New

World. Whether in *The Fur Trade in Canada*, *The Cod Fisheries* or *A History of the Canadian Pacific Railway*, we are privileged spectators to the re-enactment of history as a living tradition, to a recovery of the multiple, and layered, trajectories of the discourse of the fur trade or the cod fisheries. In Innis' writings, we can actually feel again the shock waves which erupted, and then spread out, in that first encounter of "European civilization" with the wilderness of the pre-Cambrian shield of the Northern tier of the New World. George Grant may have discussed the "will to mastery" as the primal of North America, but it is Innis who tells us, and explicitly so, what was involved in the confrontation of technique and land.

> The history of the Canadian Pacific Railroad is primarily the history of the spread of western civilization over the northern half of the North American continent. The addition of technical equipment described as physical property of the Canadian Pacific Railroad was a cause and effect of the strength and character of that civilization. The construction of the road was the result of the direction of energy to the conquest of geographic barriers. The effects of the road were measured to some extent by the changes in the strength and character of that civilization in the period following its construction.[16]

Or again, but this time with reference to the staple economy of the "fur trade":

> The history of the fur trade is the history of contact between two civilizations, the European and the North American, with especial reference to the northern portion of the continent. The limited cultural background of the North American hunting peoples provided an insatiable demand for the products of the more elaborate cultural development of Europeans. The supply of European goods, the product of a more advanced and specialized technology, enabled the Indians to gain a livelihood more easily — to obtain their supply of food, as in the case of moose, more quickly, and to hunt the beaver more effectively. Unfortunately, the rapid destruction of the food supply and the revolution in the methods of living accompanied by the increasing attention to the fur trade by which these products were secured, disturbed the balance which had grown up previous to the coming of the European. The new techno-

logy with its radical innovations brought about such a wholesale destruction of the peoples concerned by warfare and disease. The disappearance of the beaver and of the Indians necessitated the extension of European organization to the interior.[14]

The relentless conquest of "geographic barriers"; the extermination, almost indifferently, of North American civilization by "European organization"; the creation of Canadian "political union" as an administrative instrument intended to contribute to the steady expansion of an economy focussed on the extraction and exchange of "staple commodities"; the imposition of the will to empire on territory and its peoples; the reduction of the *time* of the land, and of its traditions, to an "absolute nullity": this was the real meaning of the confrontation of European technologies and the country.[18] Innis is unrelenting in his exploration of the ways in which the discourse on technology, vividly and concretely described in the commercial activities associated with the "staple commodities" of cod, lumber, pulp and paper, and fur, has shaped the Canadian identity in the New World. Perhaps more than is customary, the technological imperative is the deepest memory trace in the Canadian social heritage. The technological experience, with its European style of organization, its formative political practices in such main-line institutions as the Hudson's Bay Company (the precursor of the Canadian state),[19] its psychological habits (the "acquisitive and selfish personality"),[20] and religious practices (a mixture of pre-revolutionary Catholicism and "authoritarian" Protestantism):[21] this is the Canadian historical legacy. For Innis, technology is not something external to Canadian being; but, on the contrary, is the necessary condition and lasting consequence of Canadian existence. The Canadian discourse may be an "invention", an interrelated set of discursive practices and commerical principles, imposed on the "time" of North America: but if so, then technology is the locus of the Canadian mind. *Technique* is, in the end, the ontology, psychology, economy, and communicative ethic of the "imaginary Canadian."[22] This is to say, though, that for us, the descendants of a country formed in the image of the "staples commodity", the technological experience will always be double-edged: a horizon of domina tion surely, but also the very crucible of human emancipation. Innis said it best: we require neither the "fetishism of economy" nor the "odour of dead fish" in an over-veneration of history, but, precisely, "balance and proportion" in our appropriation of the past and future of technology.[23] Innis was a fully ambivalent thinker, oscillating between poetry and history (he often recurred to children's poetry, particularly the verses of Milne's *Winnie the Pooh*, as a way of commenting on the foibles of modern culture), because he was aware, tragically so, of the fundamental split in the Canadian mind occasioned by its creation in the image of technology. While it may be the predicament of Canadians to be, in the most constitutive sense of dependency, technological beings; then it is also the case that rethinking technology is the prime historical agency for "humanizing" not just Canadian, but North American, culture.

Indeed, Innis' literary style perfectly reflects his always bitter appreciation of Canada's destiny to be permanently, a society of the in-between: trapped between the cultural legacy of its European past and the expanding "space" of American empire. Innis' intellectual style ran to irony, satire, and invective. He was an historian who took his cultural victories where he could find them; and who, for that matter, was unsparing in his criticism of the parish history of Canadian thought. At least in his written work, Innis' use of ironic understatement and barbed words had the singular quality of evincing criticism for all, and compliments for no one. In his employment of the *mal mot*, Innis had, at least, a proper catholic sense of universalism. Thus, he was fond of speaking of the "incipient fascism" of Canadian academics who couldn't, in any case, "tell the difference between a bar association and a labour union."[24] Of Canadian politicians, Innis had this pithy, and not uninsightful, comment:

> It would be interesting to learn whether calculated stupidity has become a great political asset, but a careful study of the political leaders of Canadian parties leaves little doubt of the appearance and the reality. Perhaps political talent is inadequate to the demands of a large number of parties. In any case it would be difficult to find greater political ineptitude than exists in Canadian parties. .... Sir John A. Macdonald regarded the ideal cabinet as one over which he

> held incriminating documents such as might place each
> member in the penitentiary.[25]

And of the "fatal" influence of the "mechanized communications" of the United States on Canadian culture: "Our poets and painters are reduced to the status of sandwich men."[26] While Innis located the source of the American distemper (a country with a "complex unstable history") in its eagerness to possess the power, "but not the responsibility", of an imperialism, he traced the sickness in the Canadian mind to "the hand of puritanism."

> A counter-revolutionary tradition implies an emphasis on
> ecclesiasticism and the *ipsissima verba* of the Scriptures,
> particularly of the Old Testament with all the dangers of
> bibliolatry and of Puritanism. The hand of Puritanism is
> evident in our literature, in our art, and in our cultural life.
> This implies neglect of the interrelation of reason and
> emotion.[27]

Innis' surliness was directed with great enthusiasm against the Canadian power elite and, for that matter, against the political leadership of the American empire. In Innis' understanding, "greater realism" and "greater possibilities for delusion" are but opposite sides of the coin of modernism.[28] As he stated so eloquently in "A Plea for Time": "The shell and pea game of the country fair has been magnified and elevated to a universal level."[29] That Innis' prose style gravitated around sarcasm and bitter jibe only means, however, that he was an authentic *Canadian* thinker: a distinct psychological type which could only be produced in a society midway between privilege and dependency. Indeed, Innis' "humour" originated in that psychological intersection in the Canadian mind where awareness of (our) dependency on the cultural nullity of American empire crosses paths with a paralyzing sense of political impotence. Innis stood, where Gramsci's "organic intellectual" had been before: struck between "irresistible will" and "immovable object."[30] Innis' sarcasm, and his constant recourse to irony as an opening to the historical imagination, often took the form of an auto-critique of the hypocrisy of the Canadian bourgeois mind: a reminder to himself, and to us, of the genealogy of the Canadian way in the technocratic imperative. What, for example, could be a more telling analysis of the psychological foundations of a society intent on the commodification of almost everything than Innis' remarks on the United Empire Loyalists, the economic locus of Upper Canada.

> Generally, during the period prior to confederation, Upper Canada had developed a spirit of dependence on Great Britain which might be characterized, with no implication of condemnation, as unhealthy. The aggressive, individualistic character of its early settlers had been strengthened under the stress of circumstances and had developed especially in the trading and governing classes to the point of selfishness and acquisitiveness.[31]

But if Innis' invective assumed the proportions of a psychological *döppelganger* to the technocratic imagination, his most bitter taunts were reserved for the other side of the Canadian mind, not for its tory past but for its liberal present. Innis was the most consistent, and necessarily ineffective, of opponents against the quick absorption of Canadian society into the continentalist strategy of American empire. Indeed, it was Innis' most tragic insight that at stake in the contest of Canadian culture and American economy was nothing other than the possibility for an emancipatory recovery of the "heritage" of western civilization itself. In Innis' discourse, the reclamation, and defence, of an emergent cultural practice in Canada against the ideological hegemony of the "commercial empire" of the United States was also a sensitive political index of the struggle between "time" (duration and intension) and "space" (discontinuity and extension) in the modern mind[32]

In the fullest sense, Canada was *in* the West, but not necessarily of it; because the very "marginality" of Canadian history (the "administrative" creation of two empires and the "territorial abutment" of a third)[33] made of this society a possible agent for the recovery of the historical sense: for, that is, the remembrance, once again, of "particularity". In Innis' estimation, Canada represented in its *ideal* expression a new philosophical possibility in western civilization. The marginalization of Canada by the "metropolitan centres" of Britain, France, and the United States produced an ambivalent historical legacy: the prospect of a modern, because technological, society recovering a "living tradition" of culture by reflecting on the lessons of its European past; and, in doing so, helping to achieve "balance and proportion" between power and culture in the present century. For Innis, the true significance of Canadian society was as a possible source of a "permanent" reconciliation of the deep, and antagonistic, dualisms in western experience: time and space; culture and economy; and justice and necessity. In this reading, it was Canada's unrealized, and perhaps unrealizable fate to be the synthetic moment in the modern mind of *history* (the "commercialism" of American empire) and *poetry* (the "oral culture" of the Greeks).[34]

Much in the model of the Hippocratic tradition of medicine, ancient and modern, which he always favoured, the Canadian project in the New World was to heal the "wound" inflicted on western experience in its radical division of (technological) reason from emotion, of technique from land. Innis' discourse was, then, the historical imagination in its most magisterial statement; sweeping together into a great synthetic vision a detailed and thematic exploration of the roots of Canadian culture in its marginalization around an economy of "staples commodities", and extending this analysis into a provocative theorisation of the crisis of western civilization in the twentieth-century. Innis may have begun with a classic thesis on the dualism of "centre/margin" as the locus of the staples economy; but he eventually ended up with a highly original analysis of the dualism of "time/space" as the fundamental categories framing the crisis of twentieth-century life.[35] Innis had, indeed, "donned the mask" of technology, only to find, and this just like Proch, an ambivalent historical legacy.

Between Grant and McLuhan

But the main idea is the first one, staying alive. Canadians are forever taking the national pulse like doctors at a sickbed: the aim is not to see whether the patient will live well but simply whether he will live at all. Our central idea is

one which generates, not the excitement and sense of
adventure or danger which The Frontier holds out, not the
smugness and/or sense of security, of everything in its place
which the Island can offer, but an almost intolerable
anxiety. Our stories are likely to be tales not of those who
made it but of those who made it back, from the awful
experience — the North, the snowstorm, the sinking ship —
that killed everyone else.

M. Atwood, *Survival*

1. Survival Strategies

If Margaret Atwood is correct in her proposal that "Survival,
la survivance" is the "central symbol for Canada",[36] then Innis
is an emblematic Canadian thinker. Above all, Innis was a
technological realist: an intellectual who was interested in
examining technological experience from all sides: from the
viewpoints of power ("The Penetrative Powers of the Price
System"), culture (*The Strategy of Culture*), economic history
(*The Fur Trade in Canada*, *The Cod Fisheries*), and communicative
technologies (*The Bias of Communication*, *Empire and Communications*). And he was interested in a direct, empirical examination
of technology as a dynamic social process, not because he
wished to recover the tragic sensibility (Grant) nor because he
was a proponent of "cosmic man" (McLuhan), but for the
more prosaic, but distinctively Canadian, reason that his ideal
was that of a "stable society": a society typified by "permanence
and continuity." Innis always eschewed the dramatic polarities
of tragedy and utopia, or, what is the same, the veneration of
either "margin" or "centre", in favour of focussing his efforts
on the development of a strategy of survival, first for Canada
and then for western civilization as a whole. He was a writer
who translated the Canadian preference for "staying alive"
into a general therapeutic for the arc of contemporary societies.
Now, while a preoccupation with survival might lead, in the
beginning as well as in the end, to a highly compromised
vision of human experience, to, that is, a perspective which
grounds down the insights emanating from lament and utopia
into the grist mill of social adaptation, then it must also be said
that the realist position approximates *actual* Canadian experience. Innis was nothing if not a powerful spokesman for that
collective memory so deep in the Canadian mind of the

encounter of technique and geography. Innis' "realism" which was based on an experimental and expansively empirical approach to historical inquiry and motivated from within by the search for survival strategies was, almost literally, realist in the raw sense of the term. *The Fur Trade in Canada*, "The Wheat Economy", "Liquidity Preference", "Unused Capacity", "The Struggle Against Monopoly": these are but successive stories, across the whole sky of Canadian history, of the meeting of organism and environment: hard and brutal encounters between the people of the age of progress and the North American wilderness. Grant may write of the appropriation of the "autochthonous" and the "mastery of nature" by European settlers; but Innis' account is different. Outside the philosophical horizon of the tragic sensibility and, for that matter, entirely invisible from the viewpoint of the abstract mind of the "electronic age", there took place, in the most grim sense, a hard encounter of immigrants and the land. Disaster, menace, immiseration, and defeat were everywhere: there were a few winners (and even these, from the perspective of the "historical situation", were cogs in the structural movements of the price system), but most were losers. And as Innis has so vividly described it, the price for losing in the "new environment" was swift victimization. "Peoples who have been accustomed to the cultural traits of their civilization — what Mr. Graham Wallas calls the social heritage — on which they subsist, find it difficult to work out new cultural traits suitable to a new environment. The high death-rate of the population of the earliest European settlements is evidence to that effect."[37] In the New World at least, "depreciation of the social heritage is serious."[38] Innis provided a ground's-eye perspective on the technological experience: a story of the "creative adaptation" of European colonialists to the space and time of the New World: and, even more, in the movement from "paleotechnic capitalism" to "neotechnic capitalism" it was also a discourse on the creation of the New World Person.[39] Fittingly, Innis' rich exploration of the genealogy of technology in the "new environment" was always situated within the interstices of survival. What surfaces in his writings is a detailed account of new techniques especially adapted to the North American environment — the canoe, snowshoes, toboggans, traps, "coffin ships" — and, moreover, a range of new political practices. Innis could be such a brilliant dependency theorist because he was first a superb student of political affairs. In his writings, there is brought to life, once again, the central tensions which have typified the body politic: the hostility of the *seigneurial* system and the *coureurs de bois*;[40] the domination of western Canada by a central Canadian elite ("Western Canada has paid for the development of Canadian nationality, and it would appear that it must continue to pay. The acquisitiveness of eastern Canada shows little sign of abatement");[41] the colonization of Québec by British, and then Canadian, commercial interests; and the protracted, "tragic", dependence of the Maritime economy, subject to the "wide fluctuations" of a staples commodity, and to the "continual encirclement by capitalism."[42] Innis is the Canadian thinker who has broken generations of silence imposed by official ideology on the victims of technical dependency and class struggle in actual Canadian history. And if Innis has combined the themes of survival and technology into a complex historical tapestry, this is because Innis was an historian in the best of the realist tradition. He recorded faithfully the long traces of popular culture in Canada; and, in doing so, he was led to see, through the perspective of the immigrant experience itself, the legacy of technology as *both* centre (metropolitan domination) and margin (technological dependency as the locus of Canadian identity) in the Canadian imagination.

2. Time/Space: Breaking the Code

Harold Innis is, then, the mediation in the Canadian mind of the perspectives of technological dependency (Grant) and technological humanism (McLuhan). Innis stands midway between the tragic perspective of George Grant and the utopian imagination of Marshall McLuhan. The Innisian perspective reveals, in a way as bleak and harrowing as the visions of Grant and McLuhan, that while we are trapped within the "bias of communication" which typifies each "staples commodity", from cod fisheries (decentralized and time-bound) to television (centralized and spatialized), the technological experience also contains possibilities, if not for human emancipation, then, at least, for the recovery of civil discourse. It was Grant's contribution to think through the meaning of technique as will: his is a perspective which privileges the margin over the centre; and which, in any event, is a lament for the loss of "time" in the technological dynamo. And, on the opposite side of the Canadian mind, McLuhan was the thinker who brought to a new height of intellectual expression the perspective of technological humanism. McLuhan's ideal is the pure "space" of the electronic age; and, in direct opposition to Grant, he recognized only "centres, no margins" in the technological simulacrum. Innis' perspective is fully synthetic of Grant's "dependency" and of McLuhan's "humanism" to the extent that he privileged neither centre nor margin, but was fascinated with the dialectic of "centre/margin" as the basic tension in the culture and economy of Canadian society. And it was Innis' most original, if not most important, intellectual contribution to meditate on the problem of technology in terms of a new fusion, a new principle of "balance and proportion" between time and space. Thus to Grant's formative essay, *Time as History*, we might counter-point Innis' seminal text, "A Plea for Time". If Grant was the philosopher who in *Technology and Empire* thought most deeply about the political consequences of technology; then Innis in his book, *Empire and Communications*, explained why technology in western "civilization" runs to "monopolies of time" and "monopolies of space". And on the other side of the discourse on technology, if McLuhan in his various writings, from *Counter Blast* to *The Medium is the Massage*, unravelled the rhetorical and structural properties of electronic technologies, then Innis did even more. Not only do the essays comprising *The Bias of Communication* expand the distinction between oral and written traditions in western culture into a general theory of civilization; but Innis also succeeded, where others had failed, in breaking the genetic code of the communications discourse in western experience. In Innis' work, media of communication were examined, in brilliant historical detail, as creating "a bias in civilization favourable to an over-emphasis on the time concept or on the space concept."[43] And it was his insight that the warring tension at the heart of the "media of communication", — territory, politics, and centralization versus duration, religion, and decentralization — was precisely the fatal imbalance which led to major "cultural disturbances" in societies, classical and contemporary.[44] Thus, unlike McLuhan, Innis could never embrace, with the same enthusiasm, the vision of the new "electronic society" because his historical exploration of the "media of communication" led to the grim conclusion that the age of "cosmic man" was only another venture in a "monopoly of space." Consequently, while McLuhan could praise, with the same empty zeal as the *abstract cogito* which was always the locus of his structuralism, the mythic, participatory, and organic qualities of the technological sensorium, Innis could only remark on the "obsession with present-mindedness" (and with Wyndam Lewis: "the fashionable mind is the time-denying mind") in the modern century.[45] And while McLuhan, with an almost fatalistic sense, liked to speak of bio-technology, the slipping of the technical apparatus into the body itself, as the certain human fate in the twentieth-century, Innis was more reserved. He could speak of the recovery of "life or the living tradition"[46] because it was his theoretical, and hence political, conclusion that the time of "duration" and "intension" being the active polarity of space (discontinuity and "extension"), was also subversive of media of communication which specialized in the eye rather than the ear. But then, Innis never had to look outside the history of the "media of communication", from Sumerian culture based on the medium of clay to Semitic culture "based on the medium of stone" to the "oral tradition" of the Greeks to the "mechanized communications" of the contemporary era, for a principle of radical transformation.[47] For it was his thesis, and this never altered from his early studies in the political economy of the staples trade to his summational explorations of western civilization, that each "medium of communication" contained within its own dynamic an immanent principle of cancellation and reversal. In his estimation, the history of the media of communication was that of "centrifugal and centripetal forces": the bias of media to time or space explodes outwards in the form of the rapid organization of "monopolies of knowledge", either space-bound or time-bound; then, in a quick reversal, each medium disappears into its own vanishing-point. Or rather, in opposition to McLuhan, "the bias of one medium toward decentralization is offset by the bias of another medium toward centralization."[48] Like Grant, Innis claimed that the technological dynamo (modern culture specializes in control over space, and the cutting of time into "fragments" in industrial society) could be held in check only by a loving recovery of a sense of time (as duration) and historical continuity. As Innis said in the preface to *The Strategy of Culture* the "time concept" had to be recovered from its reduction to an "absolute nullity" at the hands of nineteenth-century thought. But unlike Grant, Innis never devoted his efforts to the reclamation of immutable justice. On the contrary, in the Innisian world, it was only by discovering a practical reconciliation between history and politics that the claims, if not of justice, then of "civilization" could be made contingent on the often violent, and always unpredictable, flow of public affairs. Innis could, and would, only speak of justice *in history*. Grant's ideal was that of the recovery of some "lost human good", of a natural justice which was sustained by a sacred presence. Innis' preoccupation was less noble, but more difficult: the creation of a "stable society,"[49] the survival of which would require a dynamic harmony between technology and culture. If, in the end, Innis adopted the strategy of social and cultural "adaptation" so reminiscent of early twentieth-century naturalists on the continent, and later of the best of American pragmatists, he also managed to maintain a sense of "religious experience", at least as articulated by the great American pragmatist, William James. For James, the religious experience was coeval with the life of active intelligence and moral conviction in the "pluralistic universe;"[50] for Innis, time, or, what was the same, the recovery of the religious sense, or some substitute thereof, against the disenchantment of the world, was tantamount to the recovery of the "oral conversations and dialectics"[51] of the early Greeks. Innis' vision of the "stable society" which held in check *power* (media of communication specializing in space) and *culture* (the readmission of the "time concept" into western politics) was also the last of the great pragmatic defences before the abyss of modern experience. In his later works, Innis would quote Nietzsche with great frequency ("In the long run, utility, like everything else, is simply a figment of our imagination and may well be the fatal stupidity by which we shall one day perish")[52] because, like James and Dewey before him, Innis took up, this time in the New World, Nietzsche's understanding that with the death of God, nihilism spreads before us. In recurring with such passionate intensity to the oral culture of the Greeks, to a civil community based on intimate face-to-face relations, Innis was, of course, restating in more classical terms the dream of an active and critical "public" which had always been the pragmatist's prescription against the nihilism of mass society. That Innisian discourse shares with John Dewey, in particular, the ideal of the democratic public, both as a political substitute for the decline of religious value and as an agency of historical transformation, only implies that technological realism may be an avant-garde expression of the pragmatic strain in North American thought.

3. Innis and the Chicago School

Now pragmatism, with its espousal of an experimental approach to social inquiry and a biological interpretation of the historical situation, is the centre of North American thought. The classic synthesis between culture and economy or, on a broader level, between the classical ideals of liberalism and the socialist critique of capitalist economy, was sought by a wide range of pragmatists in North America. To mention, for example, John Dewey and C. Wright Mills as the last and greatest of the proponents of the pragmatic tradition in the United States is only to note the dynamic centre of the American contribution to pragmatic thought. But there is also a Canadian tradition of pragmatism which reaches its zenith in the writings of Harold Innis; a Mexican variation which is represented, in part, by the critical sociology of Leopoldo Zea; and a Québécois discourse on pragmatism that is typified, and eloquently so, by the cultural sociology of Marcel Rioux.[53] Within this general, and indigenous, tradition of North American pragmatism, Innis' technological realism takes its place. But, of course, what distinguishes Innis' perspective from its American counterparts and, in a different way, from dependency perspectives in Québec and Mexico is that his thought always worked *both* sides of the radical dualism in western experience. While the claim of American pragmatism to have achieved a working synthesis of liberalism and socialism was short-

circuited, and then crushed, by the dynamo of American political power, Innis' discourse retained its vitality as a moment
of economic critique, and its promise as an opening to the
political recovery of American politics. Innis' advocacy of a
democratic public as an antidote to the nullity of the society of
mass communications was grounded historically in a philosophy
of civilization. And his searing critique of the culture of
advanced capitalist societies was based on a rich historical
understanding of the dependency relations, at the level of
economy and society, which were an essential aspect of modern
technological society. Innis was the last and best of the
"Chicago School" thinkers. While the efforts of John Dewey
and, for that matter, C. Wright Mills, to recompose a critical
"public" in the United States were doomed to failure, both by
the absence of a tradition of "civilizational discourse" in
American society and by their inability to articulate an in-
depth critique of the technological sensorium, it was different
with Innis. Because his thought developed on the *edge* of
American empire, and thus gained that necessary distance
between history (the "technological dynamo") and culture
(civilizational discourse), Innis was able to achieve what eluded
the Chicago School thinkers. In his thought, liberalism and
socialism — what C. Wright Mills has described in *The Marxists*
as the two sides of the humanist heritage in western thought[53]
— were brought together in an eloquent, comprehensive, and
powerful synthesis. Innis' perspective on technological realism
is the understanding of the inner workings of advanced capitalism, and its possible subversion, which critical thought in the
United States has always aspired to, but never succeeded in
effecting.

However, to say that Innis' critique of American empire
represents the culmination of the best political intentions of
the pragmatic tradition in the United States, and does so in a
way that does not violate his own bitter understanding as a
Canadian nationalist of "dependency" as the inner beat of
modern existence, means that the Innisian discourse relates
deeply to the two other master perspectives in the Canadian
discourse on technology. With Innis, the Chicago School may
have been alive and well in Toronto; but only because his
perspective on technology is summational of the most original

contributions of Canadian thought. Innis' critique of the "cultural disturbances" which follow in the wake of capitalism, primitive and advanced, is *so* intense because it is moved from within by an understanding of technological dependency that is as critical as Grant's. And because the Innisian discourse can zoom outwards into an exploration of the stellar system of modern communications, his understanding of the implications of modern technology was as avant-garde as McLuhan's.

4. The Technological Habitat

There are, at least, two broad thematic similarities between Innis and Grant. The Innisian imagination, just like Grant's, dwelt on *dependency* as the locus of modern empire. But while Grant concentrates on the will as the inner nucleus of technique, Innis remained an historian in the naturalist tradition. Indeed, Innis always privileged the outlook of the "biologist" in economic inquiry.[55] It was his intention, using a broad, evolutionary model of socio-economic development, to apply the properly biological principles of "growth and decay"[56] to the study of North American civilization. If the formative influences in his intellectual development included the British thinker, Graham Wallas, (*The Great Society*, *Social Judgement*, *Human Nature in Politics*) and the American theorist, Thorstein Veblen (*The Engineers and the Price System*, *Theory of the Leisure Class*), this was due to the fact that Innis was a "naturalist" in his description of the technological experience. Grant might listen for the "intimations of deprival" in technological society, and McLuhan might explore the rhetorical and purely formal laws of the media of communication, but Innis sought to explore the interstices of the *technological habitat*. And to the extent that he could discuss the "centrifugal and centripetal" tendencies in staple commodities or, by cultural extension, in each modern media of communiction, so too his dependency perspective broadened out to include an historically specific examination of the principles governing the rise and fall of each historical phase in Canada's political economy. Innis was never anything other than specific and complete. His case studies of the staple commodities, and thus of the roots of Canadian dependency, began with an understanding of each *staple*, whether newspapers, radio, fur, lumber, or cod, as an historically grounded medium of communication; with its own rhythm of economic development, with its own "timing" in relationship to the spread of the centre empires, its own class structure, and a specific relationship to its socio-natural environment.[57] With deep passion, Innis described techno-logical dependency in the most concrete of terms: the death of isolated pulp-and-paper towns as the business cycle shifts in the United States; the extermination of whole ways of life under the impact of radical innovations introduced by acce-lerating technical developments; the future obsolescence of Canada itself as its natural resources are depleted, and it is forced to assume a more complete marginalization on the periphery of American empire.[58] Innis does even more: he provides us with privileged insights into the psychology of the different technological habitats: there appears suddenly a "wheat personality", a psychology appropriate to the fur trade; a radio personality; and a psychological discourse proper to the cod fisheries.

That Innis was able to describe with such precision the historical basis, and indeed social ecology, of Canadian dependency was only because his work provided an entirely new application of the naturalistic method. Innis' "borrowings" were evident and self-announced. From Veblen, he took an understanding of "cyclonics" as well as dynamics as the central impulses of capitalist political economy.[59] And, as McLuhan notes in his introductions to *The Bias of Communication* and *Empire and Communications*, Innis was deeply influenced by the "social ecology" of Robert Parks, one of the formative members of the Chicago School. But, most importantly, all of Innis' writings bear the mark of the thought of Graham Wallas. Wallas contributed to Innis' inquiry an understanding of the dangers of "cultural astygmatism", an active appreciation of the impact of technology as the "social heritage" which encloses the imagination of its historical participants, a sensitivity to the problem of "social adaptation" as a main theme for examining the spread of European "civilization" across the North American continent, and, most of all, an understanding that each medium of communication traps us within its own specific "bias" (towards space or time).[60] Indeed, it might be said that Wallas in his fundamental writing, *Human Nature and*

Politics, provided Innis with a definition of the central intellectual problem which was to guide all of his later thinking. It
was Wallas' claim, customary in the "naturalist" tradition as it
arced around the western world, that the big problem of
western civilization was the radical scission of "reason and
emotion"[61] in modern experience since the eruption of the
modern mind in the Enlightenment. Moreover, it was Wallas'
distinct contribution, and one that was pivotal in Innis' later
writings, to show that the radical dualism between reason and
emotion (what Innis would describe as the categories of "time"
and "space") was immanent in the *social heritage*. In the end,
Wallas presented Innis not only with the challenge of attempting to discover a dynamic *principle of unification* that would heal
the *wound* in western experience; but he also forced Innis to
encounter directly the methodological proglem (the *hermeneutical* dilemma) of discovering an "epistemological" strategy by
which we might think outside of the "bias of communication"
within which we are trapped. Little wonder that Innis could
come at the Canadian experience "fresh"; and that his writings,
in their rigour and vitality, were always more than the blandishments of the economist's imagination or, to a greater extent,
more than vacant cultural criticism of American empire. Innis
could be such a brilliant political economist and communications theorist precisely because all his thought was a reflection
on the *economics, psychology, culture, and epistemology* of modern
dependency; and a continuing response to the philosophical
challenge posed, above all, by Graham Wallas. But, of course,
it was Innis' genius of intellectual expression that he was able
to supercede all of his sources, from Veblen to Wallas; absorbing
the various strands of the naturalist tradition into a dependency
theory relative to the Canadian situation. Thus, Innis provides
us with a "method" for the study of the technological habitat:
its *ontology* is the problem of technology and culture as radically
dualistic; its *epistemology* is focussed on the hermeneutical
problem of running outside and alongside cultural discourses
which are not our own; its *aesthetic* lay in the recovery of a
creative tension between the bi-polar tendencies to "time"
and "space" in modern communications; its *politics* were
directed *against* the formation of "monopolies of knowledge"
and on behalf of the pluralistic universe of civil discourse; and

its *social ecology* was focussed on the study of the multiple "adaptive strategies" by which the capitalism of the Old World was imposed on the new continent.[62] Innis may have shared with Grant a broad agreement on the relationship between technology and domination, but it was Innis' contribution to extend the dependency thesis into an exploration of the commodification of the New World. Innis never forgot that media of *communication*, whether in staples old or new, were expressions of the imposition of the commodity-form on the peoples and land of North America.

5. Empire and Civilization

If Innis shares, however ambivalently, with Grant an understanding of technology as dependency, they also have another theme in common. Innis, like Grant, always invoked a sense of historical remembrance. As the necessary counterpoint to the nihilism of the modern century, Innis could speak of *Empire and Communications* in a way similar to Grant's *Technology and Empire* because both thinkers appreciated that the question of technology summoned forth for inquiry the larger problem of power in modern life. And to the extent that Grant could speak of the power of the "technical system" as exterminatory in its impulses; so too Innis could lament the precariousness of the historical sensibility itself in the rush to technological mastery. To the same extent that Grant situated the recovery of a sense of "time" in the contemplative traditions of the Greeks, Innis also called forth the experience of the Greek city-state, and particularly in the "golden period" of Cleisthenian democracy in the fifth century B.C.[63] However, there was a singular, and decisive, difference in the two paths of recovery sketched out by Grant and Innis. While Grant wished to find in the Greeks support for an "unchanging justice", Innis wished only to locate those moments in western civilization when a creative tension was struck between the "bias of communication" in the direction of time (duration) and space (politics). Thus, while Grant would dispense with a "spatializing discourse" or, what is the same, with the recovery of an agency of historical transformation; Innis wished to rehabilitate a civilizational moment founded on a new reconciliation of time (culture) and space (government). Thus, to the extent that Innis considered "the concept of empire as an index of the efficiency of communication,"[64] then it might also be said that his search was *for* an empire in North America.

> Large-scale political organizations such as empires must be considered from the standpoint of two dimensions, those of space and time, and persist by overcoming the bias of media which over-emphasize either dimension. They have tended to flourish under conditions in which civilization reflects the influence of more than one medium and in which the bias of one medium toward decentralization is offset by the bias of another medium towards centralization.[65]

In recommending the "oral culture" of the Greeks or the vitality of the Byzantine empire at the moment of its fusion with Christianity,[66] Innis was only validating his political thesis that the operant ideal of modern society should *not* be the abolition of either "term" within our dualistic culture (neither politics nor contemplation), but rather, the *fusing* of the opposing sides of western experience (he always favoured the notion of media "offsetting" one another) into a dynamic and open-ended synthesis. In not appealing for the abandonment of the *will* which was the locus of the technological dynamo; and by not remaining sanguine about the disapperance of "particularity" in modern culture, Innis remained a technological realist to the end. But he did so in a way which required *political insurgency* if power was to be turned from within. Grant leaves us in the position of a lament beyond history and politics; Innis left us the challenge to take up anew the struggle between the ideal and historical circumstance.

6. Bio-Technology: Old and New

While Innis' discourse if fully entangled with Grant's on the two interrelated themes of technological domination and historical remembrance, the Innisian perspective also traces a great ellipse which leads directly to the technological humanism of Marshall McLuhan. Innis and McLuhan are alike in three essential respects. First, both thinkers view the technological experience through the *lens* of the development of media of communication. McLuhan explored fully the thesis that every "medium" imposes its assumptions: silently, pervasively, and structurally. The great strength, but also fatal weakness, of McLuhan's perspective was that he was always a rhetorician on the question of technology. While Innis shared with McLuhan a commitment to the study of "media of communication", his *naturalistic* approach represented a direct, and persistent, challenge to the structuralist bias of the rhetorician. Unlike McLuhan, Innis was an historian of the communications discourse, new and old. While Innis' thought never achieved the level of creativity sustained by McLuhan in his exploration of the technological discourse, it did something equally important. Innis provided an historically relative thesis on the *dialectical* relationship between the media of communication. And he was able to do so because, more than McLuhan, he had a biologist's eye for the full historical discourse surrounding the "growth and decay" of specific media of communication. Consequently, while McLuhan could discuss brilliantly the advent of the electronic age with no modesty of brush-strokes, Innis was more clinical and theoretical. Indeed, Innis' study of the "media of communication" represented an almost Weberian interpretation of the organizational strategies involved in the "imposition" and "cancellation" of the various communicative media.

There is a second major similarity between the perspectives of McLuhan and Innis: both remind us of the extent to which we are imprisoned within the sensorium of new technologies. For McLuhan technologies have a "field-effect", imposing an invisible gradient on human experience. Sudden shifts in the technological universe, from writing to printing or from the "Gutenberg Galaxy" of print technology to the new "mythic" age of video-rock, shift the ratio of the senses; causing, in fact, a radical disturbance in human perception, whether kinetic or visual. In McLuhan's discourse, biology and technology merge: the impact of electronic technology is to introduce the era of *bionic beings*, part-technique/part-flesh. This is the era of "spray-on flesh" and of bionically assisted limbs and organs. In less vivid tones, but with a vastly extended historical spectrum, it is the very same with Innis. In his introduction to *Empire and Communications*, McLuhan can write of Innis's communicative theory that it grasped the "perceptual metamorphosis"[67] of modern technologies. A single sensory shift causes massive social change. And McLuhan can note the affinity between Innis' work and his own for the reason that the investigation of technology by these two Canadian thinkers, so different in other ways, converges on a fantastic understanding of technology as a *field* of human experience. Innis writes of the "bias" of technology; and warns continually of the difficulty in breaking beyond the deep assumptions, the "astygmatism" imposed by the communicative discourse within which one is trapped.

> The significance of a basic medium to its civilization is difficult to appraise since the means of appraisal are influenced by the media, and indeed the fact of appraisal appears to be peculiar to certain types of media. A change in the type of medium implies a change in the type of appraisal and hence makes it difficult for one civilization to understand another.[68]

Just like McLuhan who noted the violence to the human organism involved in technological change, Innis said the same.

> A breach between the written and spoken word accompanied the growth of monopoly incidental to complexity of writing and invited invasion from regions in which such breaches were not in evidence and in which technological advance was unchecked.[69]

Or again, with reference to the "mechanization" of cultural experience:

> The significance of mechanization in print, photographs including the cinema, phonographs including the talkies, and radio has been evident in literature, art, and music. The pressure of mechanization on words has been reflected in simplified spelling and an interest in semantics. The limitations of words have led to resort to architecture and the rise of skyscrapers as an advertising medium.[70]

Innis and McLuhan could agree on the decisiveness of technology in precipitating massive social eruptions precisely because their discourses converged on a common understanding of the radical separation of "oral" from "written" culture as the basic break-point in western civilization. Against print culture (technologies of the "eye"), McLuhan and Innis wished to reassert the primacy of oral culture (technologies of the "ear") as the locus of civilization.[71] Consequently, McLuhan appealed often to the ideal of "blind, all-hearing Homer", and took Socrates' reflections in the *Phaedrus* as his basic text in emphasizing the difference between the "spoken word" and "writing" as the basis of modern culture. Innis, of course, appealed to exactly the same passage in the *Phaedrus* as the foundation of his thesis against written, and then print, culture.

> This discovery of yours will create forgetfulness in the learner's souls, because they will not use their memories; they will trust to the external written characters and not remember of themselves. The specific you have discovered is an aid not to memory, but to reminiscence, and you give your disciples not truth but only the semblance of truth; they will be hearers of many things and will have learned nothing; they will appear to be omniscient and will generally know nothing; they will be tiresome company, having the show of wisdom without the reality.[72]

That Innis and McLuhan share a common philosophical understanding of the significance of the loss of oral culture in western society, means also that they situate the crisis of modern civilization in the more classical terms of the suppression of poetic consciousness, and the victory of the written word, the *logos*. In the end, the thought of McLuhan and Innis represents a great curvature in the western mind: a sustained reflection on the crisis of society, which, not stopping with the material signs of that crisis, hurls itself backwards in a vast intellectual trajectory which locates finally the origins of the "crisis" in the repression of poetry, art — indeed, the mythic imagination — in western consciousness. McLuhan and Grant provide us with philosophy of civilization in the grand sense: not in the more limited terms of Mumford, Toynbee, or Kroeber; but in the tonal chords, however diverse, of Santayana, Cochrane, and Nietzsche. In the best of the tradition of Canadian thought, a tradition which also encompasses the philosophies of civilization of Charles Norris Cochrane, Dennis Lee, and Northrop Frye, Innis and McLuhan embraced the oral culture of the Greeks as a "counter-gradient" against the spatializing bias of modern technology. In the "flat-earth" society of mechanized communications, they retrieved the now forgotten oral tradition as a source of *verticality*, of duration and intrinsic value, in modern society.

But for all of the profound similarities between Innis and McLuhan they remain separated by crucial differences. Innis was always a brilliant student of public affairs; and his conclusions concerning the historical development of the "media of communication" directly reflected his economic analysis of staple commodities. There never was, anyway, such a great difference between the "staples" of cod, lumber, fur, pulp and paper and the "communicative media" of papyrus, stone, radio and television. Whether "staples" or communicative media proper, each reflected a "bias of communication", and, indeed, the "staples" in Canadian economic history were communicative media in their own right: each contained a grammar of technology which shaped communication between the New World and Europe; and each staple directly implied a "bias" towards time (the decentralization of the cod fisheries) or space (the centralization of the fur trade).[73] Consequently, it was precisely on the basis of his formative research in the Canadian staples economy that Innis was able to formulate his later conclusions (*Empire and Communications*, *The Bias of Communication*) about the decisive role of those "staples" of communication — parchment text, printing, clay tablets — in western civilization. All of the knowledge of the meeting of technique and the land acquired by Innis in his studies of Canadian political economy expand into Innis' philosophy of civilization. The significance of the St. Lawrence river in the Fur Trade in Canada parallels the primacy given by Innis to the Nile in his analysis of Egyptian culture;[74] his understanding of the "growth and decay" of the staples economy ("the ebb of commercialism was the flow of industrialism")[75] finds its reflex in his cultural analysis of the dialectical history of communicative media in western society; and what Innis discovered concerning the tendency of each commodity in the staples economy to run immediately to a "monopoly of knowledge" was exactly the same point that was later to be so central to his exploration of the relationship between power and media of communication. Innis never forgot the interrelation of power and technology; because Canadian economic history was in its essential features really a *discourse on power*. Thus, when Innis was later to write about the problem of government (control over space) in relationship to western civilization, he was only reflecting, but on a global rather than national level, what he had concluded earlier ("Transportation in the Canadian Economy", "Government Ownership and the Canadian Scene") about the intense, and necessary, involvement of the Canadian state in economic affairs. For Innis, the significance of government intervention in economic planning lay directly in its *spatial* bias: the Canadian state was a (political) corrective to the "time bias" of the landscape; it facilitated the development of "transportation" (Canadian Pacific Railway and the CNR) and "utilities" (Ontario Hydro) as a way of "offsetting" the bias inherent, both in a dependent economy and in a "discontinuous" landscape. And if later Innis was to develop a philosophy of civilization which, above all, focussed on the dangers inherent in the "rigidities" associated with either an exclusive emphasis on "time-biased" or "space-biased" media of communication, this was only a cultural reflection of the "rigidities" he had identified as the central problem of Canadian economic dependency. Finally, if Innis' communicative theory was based directly on a fascination with the "bi-polar tendencies" in the different media of communication ("centrifugal and centripetal forces")[76] this was because he had earlier explored the tension between "centre and margin" as the major dynamic of a staples economy. The theoretical premises of Innis' "economic history" are, consequently, identical to the principles which he brought to bear in his cultural exploration of the role of communicative media in western civilization. In his introductory essay in *Empire and Communications*, Innis notes that his philosophy of civilization adopts the "method" of staples analysis.[77] Innis doesn't say, however, that which is most apparent: his theory of the dialectic of "time" and "space", with their associated "monopolies of knowledge", was never anything more than an elaboration of the central tensions, and contradictions, which Innis had found in the Canadian historical situation. This naturalist used Canadian economic research as a "laboratory" for the study of civilization and empire proper; and then sharpened his understanding of the dependent nature of Canadian political economy by using the world as a laboratory for the study of Canadian/American relations; for, that is, a full exploration of the tension between time (the emergent possibility of Canadian culture) and space (the imperialist politics of the United States). In Innis' estimation, Canada's role in the New World was to civilize the politics of the United States; both as a defensive gesture on its own behalf and for other nations threatened by the "dangerous" expansionism of the American polity.[78] Thus, Innis' "strategy of culture" and his dependency theorems on the Canadian economy were always thematic aspects of a broader survival scenario: a scenario by which Canada was to play Athens to the Rome of the United States.

Civilizing America

Innis wrote dependency theory in a new key. He was capable of doing so because he never deviated from the lessons which he had learned in his study of Canadian *economic* history concerning the deep relationship between capitalism and technology; and because he never forgot the essential insight, acquired in his *political* analysis of American empire, that in an advanced capitalist society the locus of domination lies in the relationship of technology and culture. As Daniel Drache, a leading Innisian political economist, has put it: "the paradox of Canada is that it has the economic relations of an undeveloped society, but the social relations of an advanced industrial society."[79] Or, as Raymond Morrow, a contemporary social theorist, has noted: "Canada is an *advanced dependent* society."[80] As Innis, himself, said:

> We may dislike American influence, we may develop a Canadian underground movement, but we are compelled to yield to American policy. We may say that democracy has become something which Americans wish to impose on us because they say that they have it in the United States; we may dislike the assumption of Americans that they have found the one and only way of life — but they have American dollars. It may seem preposterous that North America should attempt to dictate to the cultural centres of Europe,

France, Italy, Germany, and Great Britain how they should vote and what education means — but it has American dollars.[81]

Innis was unrelenting in his analysis of the deleterious impact of American influence ("military strategy dominated by public opinion")[82] on Canadian society. He spoke continually of the "migration of technique" from the United States to Canada; of the domination "of economic trends, or perhaps we should say political trends, in Canada by political trends in the United States";[83] and he warned, in the bleakest of terms, that continued hegemony, ideological and economic, by the United States produced "conditions which seem fatal to cultural interests."[84] "We are indeed fighting for our lives"; and not only for "our lives" but also for the preservation of the traditions of western culture against the "commercial interests" of the United States. Indeed, Innis once said that "the economies of frontier countries are storm centres to the modern international economy";[85] but he might also have noted that, in his perspective, the culture of a "frontier country", like Canada, is a barometer of civilizational discourse, old and new.

If Innis could write with such accuracy about the domination of Canadian society by the commercial hegemony of American empire, it was only because his essay, "The Penetrative Powers of the Price System", had first provided a haunting description of the shock-waves suffered by Canada in the meeting of technology and capitalism in the modern economy. This essay represents, in fact, the North American equivalent of Marx's description of the "fetishism of the commodity-form." Indeed, Marx may have written of our imprisonment in the capitalist world of "abstract labour"; and of the expropriation of surplus-value from every facet of concrete existence.[86] But Innis depicted Canada itself — its cultural media, social formations, political institutions, and economy — as a *big commodity*.

The price system operated at a high state of efficiency in the occupation of the vacant spaces of the earth. In countries producing cheap and more bulky raw materials, improved transportation was dependent on funds from industrial areas. They were repaid in part in areas dominated by government

activity, such as Canada, by revenue from tariffs on manu-
factured goods from industrial areas or were avoided in part
by bankruptcy in areas dominated by private enterprise,
such as the United States.[87]

In Innis' discourse, Canada was an object-lesson in the price to
be paid in the victory of commercialism over cultural interests.
For this was a dependent society in which everything was
thrown into circulation as an object of exchange. In the fashion
of a meteorologist, Innis traced the economic development of
Canada in terms of a constant movement from high to low
pressure zones as the storm fronts of the different phases of
capitalism came into contact with one another.

> The effectiveness of the price system has been shown in the
> decline of feudalism, the decline of mercantilism, the rise of
> paleotechnic capitalism, and the shift to neotechnic capita-
> lism. It has stimulated the growth of inventions and the
> trend in the movement of goods from light and valuable raw
> materials to heavy and cheap raw materials, and to light and
> valuable finished products. It has hastened the rise of new
> sources of power and of new industries and accelerated the
> decline of obsolete regions. The drive of the price system on
> the economic and social structure within the state has been
> accompanied by continual disturbance between the states.
> The role of the state in assuming the burdens of depreciation
> through obsolescence of the wheat-coal economy and in
> stimulating the development of new industrialism involves
> rapid expansion of public debt and necessitates continual
> revision of currencies in relation to other countries.[88]

If technology is the grammar of capitalism, this is particularly
the case at the stage of "neotechnical industrialism." Like
McLuhan, but with a far more comprehensive sense of the
political economy of technology, Innis was alert to the fundamental changes occasioned in Canadian society by the shift
from mechanical to electronic sources of energy. "Neotechnic
industrialism superimposed on paleotechnic industrialism
involved changes of tremendous implication to modern
society and brought strains of great severity. The institutional
structure built up on iron and steel and coal has been slow to
change."[89] Innis was sensitive to the "tremendous implication"
of oil and hydro-electric power, the new media of the electronic

age, because he was interested, and this above all, in the *relational effects* brought about by shifts in the technical base of society. Thus he looked everywhere for the consequences of "neotechnical industrialism": in the growth of the skyscraper as the cultural landscape of modern capitalism; in the enclosure of society within the environment of the new media of mechanized communication — print, radio, and television; in the forced migration of the population into large apartment complexes; in the shift in diet from carbohydrates to vitamins or "from wheat to dairy products"; even in the effect of "improved transportation facilities of refrigeration" on increasing the range of supply of "proteins, fats, and vitamins."[90] Long before the French philosopher, Michel Foucault, said that *power* is the locus of the modern century, Innis in his studies of neotechnical capitalism had already revealed exactly *how* the power system works: by investing the body through the capillaries of diet, lifestyle, and housing; by colonizing whole societies at the level of population demographics; and by controlling the cultural apparatus of symbolization, from print technologies to radio and television.[91] When Innis described the "penetrative powers" of the price system he was serious: the subordination of Canadian society to the price system was always a more *political*, than purely economic, phenomenon. For Innis, the price system was, in fact, the language of modern power. Indeed, he could be such a brilliant interpreter of the *commodification* of Canadian society because he always knew that he was studying a society subject to the violent disturbances of the modern discourse on power. And if "Canada in the European Age"[92] was made in the image of paleotechnic capitalism; then Canada in the American Age was now subject to a discourse on power, which finally having freed itself from the constraints of "time", had now allied itself with a *commercial empire* intent on the political, if not military, control of space. But — and this is crucial — it was Innis' special insight to recognize that Canada in the American Age was exposed to a discourse on power quite unprecedented in the history of western civilization. For what was at stake in the coming-to-be of American empire was nothing less than a great *perceptual shift* in western society: the ascendancy of "monopolies of knowledge"[93] specializing in the domination of space over the traditional institutions of time. The "price system" which found its most intense expression in the "mechanized communications" (print, television, radio) of advanced capitalism, had as its final legacy the pitting of "culture versus barbarism" as the main predicament of American empire.

Without sacrificing his understanding of the political economy of "neotechnic capitalism", Innis was particularly illuminating on the question of the cultural implications of new communication technologies. And, of course, the relationship of technology and culture was so central to Innis' inquiry because he was convinced that neotechnic capitalism, by emphasizing communication technologies which specialized exclusively in the colonization of space had also precipitated a profound crisis of civilization. In a series of essays ranging from "The Problem of Space", "Industrialism and Cultural Values", "Technology and Public Opinion in U.S.A." to "The Strategy of Culture", Innis outlined in broad brush-strokes the civilizational crisis that had erupted with the innovation of the electronic media.[94] Thus, for example, in "The Problem of Space", he undertook a highly original and provocative historical survey of the dialectic of space (existence) and time (an order of succession) in western culture. His conclusion, that with the coming of print technology in industrial society the "destruction of time" and the "oral tradition" was assured, served as a theoretical prelude to the critique of industrialism offered in "Industrialism and Cultural Value." In this essay, Innis was concerned with a diagnosis of the "disasters which overtook North American civilization following the coming of Europeans."

> The concern with specialization and excess, making more and better mousetraps, precludes the possibility of understanding a preceding civilization concerned with balance and proportion. Industrialism implies technology and the cutting of time into precise fragments suited to the needs of the engineer and the accountant. The inability to escape the demands of industrialism time weakens the possibility of an appraisal of limitations of space. Constant changes in technology particularly as they affect communication, a crucial factor in determining cultural values . . . increase the difficulties of recognizing balance let alone acheive it.[95]

Innis could be so caustic on the claims to "superiority" of machine culture just because he brought to bear the more ancient standard of Greek civilization. "In contrast with the civilization dominated by Greek culture with its maxim 'nothing in excess', modern civilization dominated by machine industry is concerned with specialization which might be described as always in excess."[96] Not satisfied, though, to arraign the ethical standards of the oral culture of the Greeks against American empire, Innis also undertook an historically specific study of the media of communication in advanced capitalist societies. His empirical studies extended across the newspaper, telegraph, printing press, radio, and magazines, but, of course, always with the theoretical intention of relating the emergence of "mechanized communication" to the dissolution of an embodied sense of time. Thus, in "Technology and Public Opinion in U.S.A.", Innis noted:

> Schumpeter in his *Business Cycles* has emphasized the importance of the Kondratieff cycle but has neglected the problem of organization of communication by which innovations are transmitted. As monopoly of communication with relation to the printing press built up over a long period under the protection of freedom on the press, accentuated discontinuity and the destruction of time, it eventually destroyed itself and compelled a recognition of a medium emphasizing time and continuity. Veblen's emphasis on the pecuniary and industrial dichotomy overlooks the implications of technology, for example in the printing industry, and its significance to the dissemination of information in a pecuniary society. A monopoly which accentuates more rapid dissemination brings about a profound disruption of society.[97]

It was on the basis of a broadly conceived historical survey of new communication technologies that Innis approached the question of the *culture crisis* provoked by the ideological hegemony of American empire, together with its implications for Canada. Innis admitted, at once, that his bias was with "the oral as against the mechanized tradition" and that, in his estimation, the modern crisis of culture is such that "The conditions of freedom of thought are in danger of being destroyed by science, technology and the mechanization of knowledge, and with them, Western civilization."[98] And nowhere were the effects of "mechanized communication" more "pernicious" than in the Canadian cultural discourse. In "The Strategy of Culture", Innis developed a remarkable cultural interpretation, both of the growth of mass communication technologies as the dynamic centre of American empire, and the intimate relationship between the politics of imperialism and ideological hegemony in American history. Operating on the political assumption that "what we don't know will hurt us",[99] Innis provided an entirely persuasive, and bleak, account of the historical relationship between expansive militarism and electoral politics in American history; and, moreover, of the use by the command-centres of the United States of the media of "mechanized communication" as instruments of power. Innis' political lesson was clear: the United States was now a fully "space-oriented" society, with no inner coordinating principle and with no organic conception of "lived tradition", time, succession, or duration which might act as an inner check against the politics of imperialism. In the American mind, there came together an historical tilt in favour of the violence of militarism (as a truth-sayer of the sectional cleavages of domestic politics) and a cultural bias in favour of media of communication oriented to the control of space. The United States could be the lead empire of the modern age because its internal political history, and its "will" to imperialism (founded on "missionary consciousness"),[100] predisposed it to take full advantage of the "bias of communication" towards the abolition of tradition, and the ascendency of the politics of spatial control.

Confronted with an American empire, fully expressive of the lead tendencies of modern culture ("mechanized communication" and the politics of spatial domination), the Canadian situation is precarious. Citing "conditions which seem fatal to cultural interests", Innis recommended a survival strategy which emphasized taking "persistent action at strategic points against American imperialism in all its attractive disguises ... (b)y attempting constructive efforts to explore the cultural possibilities of various media of communication and to develop them along lines free from commercialism."[101] Innis' survival strategy, with its emphasis on cultural emancipation and on the de-commercialization of technology, was moderate in the face of the challenge of American empire. "The overwhelming pressure of mechanization evident in the newspaper and the magazine has led to the creation of vast monopolies of communication. Their entrenched positions involve a continuous, systematic, ruthless destruction of elements of permanence essential to cultural activity."[102] But then, Innis' concern was with the emancipatory vision which he had outlined in "A Plea for Time", with its highly nuanced understanding of the different "forms" of time (biological, social, intellectual) and its tragic recommendation that only in a retrieval of some balance between duration and space could the crisis of modern civilization be recovered. Canada was to be "A Plea of Time" against "The Problem of Space" of the United States. Innis was nothing if not a pragmatic realist, and a thinker who refused the comforting lie. Thus he concluded "The Strategy of Culture" with this searing insight into the limited emancipatory material in Canadian politics. "We have never had the courage of a Yugoslavia in relation to Russia and we have never produced a Tito. We have responded to the demands of the United States sometimes with enthusiasm and sometimes under protest.... (W)e have been a part of the North American continent."[103] Innis was then a technological realist: he sought to preserve some critical space in Canadian discourse for the recovery of an authentic sense of time, while recognizing that it was Canada's destiny, under the technological sway of the United States, to occupy in "North America the place of Czechoslavakia as a show window in relation to Russia in Europe, first as to the British Empire and second as to the American Empire."[104] There can be, perhaps, no better reflection on Canada's predicament in the civilizational crisis produced by the neotechnical capitalism of the United States than to recall the words of Lewis Carroll which Innis himself was so fond of quoting.[105]

> He thought he saw a banker's clerk
> Descending from a bus,
> He looked again and saw it was
> A hippopotamus.
> "If this should stay to dine" he said
> "There won't be much for us."

5

Epilogue:
Technology and Culture

The Eclipse of Culture

The modern century is fully ambiguous, charged with opposing tendencies towards domination and freedom, radical pessimism and wild optimism.

Under the pressure of rapid technological change, the centre may no longer hold but this just means that everything now lies in the balance between catastrophe *or* creation as possible human destinies. Indeed, central to the human situation in the twentieth-century is the profound *paradox* of modern technology as simultaneously a prison-house and a pleasure-palace. We live now with the great secret, and the equally great anxiety, that the technological experience is both Orwellian and hopelessly utopian. Exhibiting as it does conflicting tendencies towards emancipation and manipulation, technological society presents us with the fateful, but opposing, models of the engineer and the artist as ways of relating to the new society of technique.

With the smell of exterminism in the air, we have reached a fantastic cusp in human history. In most practical and terrifying sense, we are now either at the end of history or, just possibly, at the beginning of all things. Left to its own imperatives, technological experience is just dangerous enough as to force us, almost in spite of ourselves, to rethink the deep relationship of technology and civilization. Literally, if we are to survive as a species, it will be due in no small part to the terrible fact that the sheer extremity of the threat to the human species posed by the new technologies (the Bomb as the sign of twentieth-century experience) will have forced a dramatic revaluation of human ethics. If it is much too optimistic to expect that the Bomb will force us to exercize a new sense of inner restraint in public affairs; then it still might be said that the Bomb has, at least, this great paradoxical effect. On the other side of exterminism, there exists now the objective conditions for a new, universal human culture. The Bomb, just because it is global in consequence, compels us to think of ethics from a universal standpoint. And on the other side of the silicon chip is the, admittedly dim, possibility of a new information order. Technology may not force us to be free; but it does encourage us to rethink the relationship of technique, ethics, and society.

Seemingly then, this is one of those great transitional periods in which technological innovations, in diverse areas ranging from computers, silicon chips, prosthetic medicine and video to nuclear armaments, have suddenly leaped beyond our ability to understand the connection between such new technologies and past events, or to foresee their possible consequences. If this is an age of such great social anxiety and stress, then it is so, in good part, because there is now such a radical separation between the swift tempo of public events, based as they are on the rapid unfolding of the logic of the technological imperative, and private life which still works off of traditional habits of perception. We're either "book people" in an age which privileges video or, just when we have adapted to the new realities of electronic circuitry as the model of contemporary politics and society, suddenly electronics itself is made obsolete by the digital revolution! It's as if everything is out of synch: a society with twenty-first century engineering, but nineteenth-century perception.

Indeed, it is apparent, now more than ever, that we are living in the midst of a terrible *ethics gap*: a radical breach between the realities of the designed environments of the new technologies, and the often outmoded possibilities of our private and public moralities for taking measure of the adequacy of technological change. It's as if we live in a culture with a super-stimulated technical consciousness, but a hyper-atrophied moral sense. It is just this gap between ethics and technology which makes it so difficult to render meaningful judgments on specific technological innovations in satisfying or thwarting the highest social ideals of western culture. Just like "jet lag" in which the psychological consequences of life in the mainstream of technology are experienced only *after* the event is finished; "ethics lag" means that we are blindsided on the real effects of technology until it is too late. What is our practical situation now? It's just this: technology without a sustaining and coherent ethical purpose; and ethics, public and private, without a language by which to rethink technology in late twentieth-century experience.

In ways more pervasive than we may suspect, technology is now the deepest language of politics, economy, advertising, and desire. We may not be seduced by television, but it's the image-system at the centre of a burgeoning world culture in lifestyles, fashion and consumer ideology. We may be depressed by the Bomb, but it's the information medium which is shaping and reshaping the politics of the modern century. We may not want to take video rock seriously, but it's the dynamic locus of an expanding and homogenous world environment of sound/images: a type of popular culture which works in the language of violence, pornography, and seduction. And, finally, we might like to consider personal computers as just the flip side of electronic typewriters until we wake up one day in a society modelled on the pattern of Computerino, U.S.A. and realize that it's *we* who are being processed into the information bytes of the mass communication system. In *The Gutenberg Galaxy*, McLuhan had this to say of the cultural impact of the new

technologies of communication: "How are you to reason with
a person who feeds himself into the buzz-saw just because the
teeth are invisible?" When television can be used to pump the
mass full of advertising messages and their associated emotions;
when overnight polling can detect any blips in the mood of the
population; when the everyday occurence of transistorized
consumers walking to the beat of their Sony Walkman's is a
grisly example of *us* as the bytes of the information society:
then we are not far from the invisible teeth of McLuhan's
"buzz-saw".

The special contribution of Innis, McLuhan and Grant
does not lie just in what they have to tell us about the *practical
workings* of the wired society. Innis got to the age of radio, but
not beyond it; Grant always remained a print man; and
McLuhan, while the most experimental of the three, was by
virtue of historical circumstance never able to see beyond
electronic society to the digital manipulations of the silicon
chip.[1] The relentless speed-up of the pace of technological
change which McLuhan could only prophecy has now taken
place. We are fully modern beings just because the technological media "horizon" us on all sides now. Innis, McLuhan
and Grant might concur that "technology is the real world";
but it is a distinctively modern fate to *live* technology as a kind
of second biology which, whether in city architecture,
chemically processed foods, sound production or the zooming
lens of the camera eye, defines and limits the human condition.
In terms of the sheer scale and acceleration of technological
change, it's as if we are forever separated from McLuhan, Innis
and Grant by a new continental divide. This generation of
thinkers might have brought us to the edge of the technological dynamo, but it's our fate now to experience the designed
environments of technology as *the* most pervasive and basic
fact of human existence. And unlike, for example, the beginnings of that other, great technical paradigm-shift prefigured
by the industrial revolution, which was marked anyway by a
violent and easily discernible *mechanization* of the institutions
of agrarian society, the new technologies of communication
imprint themselves instantaneously and universally on human
consciousness. When *Dallas* becomes a global cultural item;
when the Cruise Missile comes to rest in the English country-
side and in the Canadian North; when Love Canal and acid rain

are everywhere; when Michael Jackson, Boy George, and Men Without Hats explode outwards like new cultural stars in a global media system which works its economic magic in an entirely new, and as yet little understood, grammar of video images and technically manipulated emotions: then it's time for a new Copernican Revolution in thinking technology.

For us, politics can now be so cynical just because it is shadowed by the logic of exterminism; ethical questions concerning human reproduction are screened out by rapid advances in genetic engineering; video rock has become the most dynamic literature of the last decades of the twentieth-century; and television is important to study because it provides the basic, visual language of contemporary popular culture. If it is fair to note, and this following the Polish thinker Leszek Kolakowski, that every crisis contains both a moment of danger *and* opportunity, then it must also be said that it is part of the modern circumstance in North America to live just between the dark side of the "chip" and the new morning of global communications. In a fundamental sense, we can never go home again to the texts of McLuhan, Innis and Grant; but we must turn now to decipher the human predicament in the New World. The Québec film-maker, Jean-Claude Labrecque, once said of the threat of cultural obliteration posed by the new technologies of communication: "It's like snow: it keeps falling and all you can do is go on shovelling".[2] Technology as snow, or maybe as a nuclear winter; that's the Canadian, and by extension, world situation now. If we wish to survive cultural extermination, then our main chance is just what Labrecque says: "we must be original or disappear". Jean-Paul Sartre might have cautioned the Europeans that they were "condemned to be free" as the price of modernism; but Labrecque notes that the Canadian fate is simply this: "create or perish".

With and beyond the discourse of Innis, McLuhan and Grant, *our* political problem is just this. In the world of the silicon chip, there are no centres and no margins. Everyone is peripheralized now by the systemic logic of technological society. There is no centre which is not undergoing a fantastic reversal into decay and annihilation. If the politics of the silicon chip represent the end-point of the reflections of Innis, McLuhan and Grant, then this just means that their ending is our beginning.

Notes

1

1. Maurice Charland, "Technological Nationalism", in *Technology, Culture and Power: A Canadian Discourse, CJPST/New World Perspectives*, forthcoming, fall, 1985.

2. Marcel Rioux, *Québec in Question*, Toronto: Lorimer, 1978, p.187.

3. See particularly: Margaret Atwood, *Survival: A Thematic Guide to Canadian Literature,* Toronto: Anansi, 1972 *and* Dennis Lee, *Savage Fields: An Essay in Literature and Cosmology*, Toronto: Anansi, 1977.

4. Dallas Smythe, *Dependency Road: Communications, Capitalism, Consciousness and Canada*, Norwood, N.J: Ablex Publishers, 1981; and Patricia M. Marchak, *In Whose Interests: An Essay on Multinational Corporations in a Canadian Context*, Toronto: McClelland and Stewart, 1979.

5. The Canadian discourse on technological humanism extends from the fields of literary criticism to communication studies to political theory, wherever, in fact, *liberalism* is the animating vision and the horizon within which the perspective on technology is couched. See especially, (in political theory) Pierre E. Trudeau, *Federalism and the French Canadians*, Toronto: Macmillan of Canada, 1968; (in literary criticism) Northrop Frye's writings from *The Modern Century*, Toronto: Oxford University Press, 1967 and *The Educated Imagination*, Toronto: Canadian Broadcasting Corporation, 1963, to *Creation and Recreation*, Toronto: Canadian Broadcasting Corporation, 1980 and *The Bush Garden: Essays on the Canadian Imagination,* Toronto: Anansi, *1971.* Finally, for a leading exponent of technological humanism, see Eric Havelock's *Prometheus*, Seattle: University of Washington Press, 1968 and *Preface to Plato*, Cambridge: Harvard University Press, 1963.

6. See particularly, Mel Watkins, *Dene Nation: The Colony Within*, Toronto: University of Toronto Press, 1977; Wallace Clement, *Continental Corporate Power: Economic Elite Linkages Between Canada and the United States*, Toronto: McClelland and Stewart, 1977; Daniel Drache, "Rediscovering Canadian Political Economy", in *A Practical Guide to Canadian Political Economy*, edited by Wallace Clement and Daniel Drache, Toronto: Lorimer, 1978, pp. 1-53.

7. Eli Mandel, *Contexts of Canadian Criticism*, Chicago: University of Chicago Press, 1971; Margaret Laurence, *The Diviners*, Toronto: McClelland and Stewart, 1978; *The Fire-Dwellers*, New York;

Knopf, 1969; *A Jest of God*, Toronto: McClelland and Stewart, 1974; and *The Stone Angel*, London, Ont: Gatefold Books, 1980; and Alice Munro, *The Moons of Jupiter*, Toronto: Macmillan of Canada, 1982 and *Dance of the Happy Shades*, Toronto: Ryerson Press, 1968.

2

1. Grant's most existential account of the language of deprival at the centre of technological society is to be found in his essay, "A Platitude", *Technology and Empire: Perspectives on North America*, Toronto: House of Anansi, 1969, pp. 137-143. Grant's most searing account on the "nihilistic will to will" as the animating vision of modern technical society is provided in his brilliant text, *Time as History*, Toronto: Canadian Broadcasting Corporation, 1969, pp. 31-43.

2. G. Grant, *Technology and Empire*, pp. 17-18.

3. *Ibid.*, p. 138.

4. *Ibid.*

5. *Ibid.*, p. 40.

6. *Ibid.*, p. 138.

7. G. Grant, *Time as History*, p. 31.

8. Grant's criticism of the "creative leadership" of the "realised technological society" ranges from the political to the philosophical. For a directly political account of the dependent character of Canadian liberalism, see Grant's *Lament For a Nation: The Defeat of Canadian Nationalism*, Toronto: McClelland and Steward, 1965. For a philosophical meditation on the linking of willing and knowledge in the nihilism of modern politics, see *Time as History*, p. 19.

9. Friedrich Nietzsche, *The Will to Power*, translated by Walter Kaufman and R.J. Hollingdale, New York: Vintage, 1968.

10. As Nietzsche said in *The Will to Power*, "The deeper one looks, the more our valuations disappear — meaninglessness approaches.", p. 326.

11. *Ibid.*, p. 356.

12. G. Grant, *Technology and Empire*, p. 137.

13. *Ibid..*

14. *Ibid..*

15. *Ibid.*, p. 139.

16. *Ibid.*

17. See particularly, Theodor Adorno and Max Horkheimer's essay on "The Culture Industry" in *Dialectic of Enlightenment*, New York: Hesder and Hesder, 1972, pp. 120-167.

18. This theme returns in Dennis Lee's *Savage Fields*.

19. G. Grant, *Technology and Empire*, p. 15.

20. *Ibid.*, p. 28.

21. *Ibid.*, p. 138.

22. Grant's image of bionic beings finds its most powerful expression in his essay, "A Platitude" in *Technology and Empire*.

23. G. Grant, *Technology and Empire*, p. 142.

24. *Ibid.*, p. 141.

25. *Ibid.*

26. *Ibid.*, p. 143.

27. Barrington Moore, Jr., *Social Origins of Dictatorship and Democracy: Lord and Peasant in the Making of the Modern World*, Boston: Beacon Press, 1966.

28. G. Grant, *Lament for a Nation*, p. 47.

29. *Ibid.*, p. 68.

30. *Ibid.*, pp. 69-70.

31. *Ibid.*, p. 76.

32. In Grant's vision, consumption is the dynamic locus of modern culture. An ethic of consumption is, in fact, the vacant moral principle of *liberal* society.

33. G. Grant, *Lament for a Nation*, p. 80.

34. *Ibid.*

35. *Ibid.*

36. G. Grant, *Time as History*, p. 33.

37. G. Grant, *Philosophy in the Mass Age*, Toronto: Copp Clark, 1959, pp. 2-3.

38. G. Grant, *Lament for a Nation*, p. 74.

39. *Ibid.*, pp. 76-85.

40. *Ibid.*, p. 2.

41. *Ibid.*, p. 4.

42. *Ibid.*, p. 3.

43. G. Grant, *Lament for a Nation*, p. 5.

44. G. Grant, *Philosophy in the Mass Age*, p. 100.

45. *Ibid.*.

46. G. Grant, *Lament for a Nation*, p. 4.

47. *Ibid.*, p. 3.

48. G. Grant, *Philosophy in the Mass Age*, p. 3.

49. For Grant, the Great Lakes region is the dynamic centre of the technological society of North America.

50. All of Grant's writings are an acount, though from different angles of visions, on technological liberalism. *English-Speaking Justice* is an interpretation of the liberal account of justice; *Philosophy in the Mass Age* is an interpretation of the moral theory which informs the liberal imagination; and *Time as History* examines the "will to will" as the philosophical animus of political liberalism.

51. G. Grant, *English-Speaking Justice*, Sackville, New Brunswick: Mount Allison University, 1974, p. 78.

52. G. Grant, *Time as History*, p. 15.

53. *Ibid.*, p. 18.

54. *Ibid.*, p. 8.

55. Grant's essential contribution to the discourse on technology has to do with this meditation on its "foundational categories".

56. *Ibid.*, p. 52.

57. G. Grant, *Philosophy in the Mass Age*, pp. 14-27.

58. *Ibid.*, p. 42.

59. *Ibid.*

60. *Ibid.*

61. *Ibid.*, p. 20.

62. *Ibid.*, p. 20.

63. G. Grant, *English-Speaking Justice*, p. 91.

64. *Ibid.*

65. *Ibid.*

66. *Ibid.*, p. 88.

67. *Ibid.*, pp. 88-89.

68. *Ibid.*, p. 89.

69. *Ibid.*

70. *Ibid.*, p. 84.

71. *Ibid.*

72. *Ibid.*

73. *Ibid.*, p. 83.

74. See particularly, Grant's, *Philosophy in the Mass Age*, pp. 42-53.

75. *Ibid.*, p. 84.

76. *Ibid.*, pp. 84-85.

77. *Ibid.*, p. 93.

78. *Ibid.*, p. 54.

79. *Ibid.*, p. 55.

80. *Ibid.*, p. 54.

81. George Grant, *Time as History,* p. 44.

82. *Ibid.*, p. 33.

83. *Ibid.*

84. In Grant's discourse, liberalism is the ideology of the "creative leaders" who continue to act in the midst of the death of the social.

85. *Ibid.*, p. 34.

86. *Ibid.*, pp. 39-41.

87. *Ibid.*, p. 38.

88. *Ibid.*

89. G. Grant, *Philosophy in the Mass Age*, pp. 98-112.

90. G. Grant, *Time as History*. p. 48.

91. M. Weinstein, *The Wilderness and the City: American Classical Philosophy as a Moral Quest*, Amherst: University of Massachusetts Press, 1982, pp. 69-89.

92. See also, R. Barthes, *The Pleasure of the Text*, translated by Richard Miller, New York: Hill and Wang, 1975, p. 34.

93. G. Grant, *Time as History*, p. 41.

3

1. H.A. Innis, *Empire and Communications*, Toronto: University of Toronto Press, 1972, pp. 1-2.

2. M. McLuhan, *Understanding Media: The Extensions of Man*, Toronto: McGraw-Hill, 1964, p. 2.

3. The image of the "probe" runs through all of McLuhan's writings, from *Understanding Media* to *The Medium is the Massage*.

4. M. McLuhan, "Catholic Humanism & Modern Letters", *Christian Humanism in Letters*, Hartford, Connecticut: St. Joseph's College, 1954, p. 78.

5. M. McLuhan, *Counter Blast*, Toronto: McClelland and Stewart, 1969, p. 42.

6. The relationship of *Empire, Inc.* to the Canadian imagination was first developed by Michael Dorland in a brilliant essay, "Power, TV & the National Question: A Reproach", *Symposium on Television & Popular Culture*, Queen's University, March 2, 1983.

7. McLuhan's most vivid description of the "technological sensorium" is provided in his writing, *The Medium is the Massage*. (with Quentin Fiore), New York: Bantam, 1967, p. 26.

8. M. McLuhan, *Counter Blast*, p. 14.

9. For McLuhan's extended analysis of the movie as a "mechanizing" medium see "The Reel World", *Understanding Media*, pp. 284-296.

10. McLuhan also described the telegraph as a "social hormone", *Understanding Media*, pp. 246-257.

11. M. McLuhan, *Counter Blast*, p. 16.

12. M. McLuhan, *The Medium is the Massage*, p. 26.

13. M. McLuhan, *Counter Blast*, p. 14.

14. *Ibid.*, p. 31.

15. *Ibid.*, p. 30.

16. *Ibid.*, p. 26.

17. *Ibid.*, p. 41.

18. *Ibid.*, p. 14.

19. *Ibid.*, pp. 22-23.

20. M. McLuhan, *Understanding Media*, p. 51.

21. M. McLuhan, "A Historical Approach to the Media", *Teacher's College Record*, 57(2), November, 1955, p. 110.

22. *Ibid.*, p. 109.

23. *Ibid.*, p. 110.

24. M. McLuhan, *Through the Vanishing Point: Space in Poetry and Painting*, New York: Harper and Row, 1968, p. 181.

25. *Ibid.*

26. *Ibid.*, pp. 24-25.

27. *Ibid.*, p. 24.

28. *Ibid.*, p. 25.

29. *Ibid.*, p. 24.

30. *Ibid.*

31. *Ibid.*, p. 181.

32. The arts as "radar feedback" is a major theme of *Understanding Media*. See particularly, the introductory comments, pp. vii-xi.

33. M. McLuhan, *Through the Vanishing Point*, p. 21.

34. M. McLuhan, *Counter Blast*, p. 31.

35. See particularly, M. McLuhan, *The Mechanical Bride: Folklore of Industrial Man*, New York: The Vanguard Press, 1951.

36. McLuhan wrote in *Understanding Media*, "To put one's nerves outside, and one's physical organs inside the nervous system, or brain, is to initiate a situation — if not a concept — of dread". p. 222.

37. McLuhan's most expansive statement on the relationship of the Catholic mind to the study of modern civilization is located in his article, "Catholic Humanism & Modern Letters".

38. M. McLuhan, *The Medium is the Massage*, p. 68.

39. Jean Baudrillard, *L'échange symbolique et la mort*, Paris: Éditions Gallimard, 1976, pp. 89-95.

40. McLuhan's sense of communications as a new universalism is a unifying theme across his texts, from *The Medium is the Massage* to *Understanding Media* and *Counter Blast*. It was also a Catholic ethic which was at work in his thought about the media.

41. M. McLuhan, "Catholic Humanism and Modern Letters", p. 75.

42. *Ibid.*, p. 74.

43. *Ibid.*, p. 80.

44. *Ibid.*, pp. 75-76.

45. *Ibid.*, p. 75.

46. *Ibid.*, pp. 82-83.

47. *Ibid.*, p. 80.

48. Indeed, McLuhan describes the "new media" of communication (... as ...) magical art forms, "Catholic Humanism and Modern Letters", p. 79.

49. M. McLuhan, *The Medium is the Massage*, p. 69.

50. M. McLuhan, *Understanding Media*, p. 56.

51. M. McLuhan, *The Medium is the Massage*, p. 120.

52. *Ibid.*, p. 114.

53. See particularly, M. McLuhan, *Counter Blast*, p. 42.

54. M. McLuhan, *Understanding Media*, p. 64.

55. *Ibid.*, p. 56.

56. M. McLuhan, "An Ancient Quarrel in Modern America" in *The Interior Landscape: The Literary Criticism of Marshall McLuhan, 1943-62*, edited by Eugene McNamara. Toronto: McGraw-Hill, 1969, p. 231.

57. M. McLuhan, "Joyce, Aquinas, and the Poetic Process", *Renascence* 4(1), Autumn, 1951, pp. 3-4.

58. *Ibid.*, p. 3.

59. *Ibid.*

60. *Ibid.*, p. 7.

61. *Ibid.*, p. 4.

62. *Ibid.*, p. 5.

63. *Ibid.*

64. *Ibid.*, p. 9.

65. *Ibid.*, p. 8.

66. M. McLuhan and Quentin Fiore, *The Medium is the Massage*, p. 151.

67. For an illuminating account of the significance of Thucydides' epistemology to modern consciousness, see Charles Cochrane, *Thucydides and the Science of History*, Oxford: Oxford University Press, 1929.

68. See particularly, M. McLuhan's "Joyce, Acquinas and the Poetic Process", p. 3, and "Catholic Humanism and Modern Letters", p. 72.

69. McLuhan's understanding of the creative possibilities of "simultaneity" and "instantaneous scope" is developed in *The Medium is the Massage*.

70. While McLuhan analyzes the phenomenon of "closure" in many of his writings, this concept is the locus of *Counter Blast* and *Understanding Media*.

71. M. McLuhan, *Understanding Media*, p. 26.

72. M. McLuhan, *Counter Blast*, p. 5.

73. *Ibid.*, p. 42.

74. *Ibid.*

75. *Ibid.*

76. *Ibid.*

77. *Ibid.*, p. 62.

78. M. McLuhan, *Understanding Media*.

79. *Ibid.*, p. 42.

80. *Ibid.*

81. *Ibid.*

82. *Ibid.*, p. 43.

83. See particularly, M. McLuhan, *Understanding Media*, p. 42, and *Counter Blast*, p. 17.

84. M. McLuhan, *Understanding Media*, p. 43.

85. *Ibid.*, p. 252.

86. *Ibid.*

87. *Ibid.*, p. 142.

88. McLuhan always counterposed the mythic, inclusive and in-depth viewpoint to the homogeneity of visual culture.

89. This was a main thematic of *The Medium is the Massage*, pp. 112-117.

90. *Ibid.*, p. 120.

91. M. McLuhan and Quentin Fiore, *The Medium is the Massage*, p. 142.

92. See especially, M. McLuhan, *Understanding Media*, p. 68.

93. *Ibid.*

94. *Ibid.*

95. *Ibid.*, p. 80.

96. *Ibid.*, p. 141.

97. M. McLuhan, "The Relation of Environment & Anti-Environment", in F. Marsen's *The Human Dialogue: Perspectives on Communications*, New York: The Free Press, 1967, p. 43.

98. Charles Norris Cochrane, "The Latin Spirit in Literature", *University of Toronto Quarterly*, Vol. 2, No. 3, (1932-33), pp. 315-338.

99. Professor Andrew Wernick coined this term in describing the interplay of power/media in the thought of the contemporary French social theorist, Jean Baudrillard.

4

1. For a brilliant exploration of four Manitoba painters (Esther Warkov, Tony Tascona, Ivan Eyre and Don Proch) see Kenneth J. Hughes, *Manitoba Art Monographs*, Government of Manitoba, Department of Cultural Affairs and Historical Resources, 1982.

2. This warning by E. Carpenter was also a basic theme in M. McLuhan's *Understanding Media*.

3. See, K.J. Hughes, *Manitoba Art Monographs*, p. 95.

4. Karyn Allen, *The Winnipeg Perspective, 1981: Ritual*, p. 12.

5. H.A. Innis, *Essays in Canadian Economic History*, edited by Mary Q. Innis, Toronto: University of Toronto Press, 1956, p. 392.

6. Innis' classic account of the counter-revolutionary tradition in Canadian politics is contained in his essay, "The Church in Canada", *Essays in Canadian Economic History*, pp. 383-393.

7. Innis described the cultural implications of "neo-technical industrialism" in two superb essays: *The Strategy of Culture*, Toronto: University of Toronto Press, 1952; "A Plea for Time", in *The Bias of Communication*. Toronto, University of Toronto Press, 1951, pp. 61-91. Innis' account of "spatially biased media of communication" is presented most forcefully in two other essays, "The Problem of Space" and "Industrialism and Cultural Values", both of which are included in *The Bias of Communication*.

8. For a summational statement on the development of Canada as an appendage of empire, see H.A. Innis, "Great Britain, The

United States and Canada", in *Essays in Canadian Economic History*, pp. 395-412.

9. H.A. Innis, *The Bias of Communication*, p. 141.

10. H.A. Innis, *Essays in Canadian Economic History*, p. 157.

11. H.A. Innis, *The Bias of Communication*, p. 91.

12. *Ibid.*, p. 141.

13. See particularly, H.A. Innis, *The Strategy of Culture*, pp. 18-20.

14. H.A. Innis, *The Bias of Communication*, p. 62.

15. Innis' most remarkable and original insight is that the tension between media of *time* and media of *space* is a reflex of the centre/margin thesis in Canadian economic history. For a full account of his time/space theory, the following two essays should be read as parallel, but reverse, images of one another: "A Plea for Time" (61-91) and "The Problem of Space" (92-131), in *The Bias of Communication*.

16. H.A. Innis, *A History of the Canadian Pacific Railway*, Toronto: University of Toronto Press, 1971, p. 287.

17. H.A. Innis, *The Fur Trade in Canada*, New Haven: Yale University Press, 1930, p. 392.

18. The thematic which unifies all of Innis' writings, from *The Cod Fisheries* and *The Fur Trade in Canada* to *The Strategy of Culture* is the fateful association of technology and empire in the formation of Canadian society. Innis could speak of time as an "absolute nullity" (*The Strategy of Culture*) and of the exterminism of the native population (*The Fur Trade in Canada*) just because he understood that power is the locus of modern empire.

19. Paul Phillips, "The State and the Economy", *Canadian Journal of Political and Social Theory*, Vol. I, No. 3, 1977, p. 74.

20. H.A. Innis, *The Fur Trade in Canada*, pp. 290-294.

21. H.A. Innis, *Essays in Canadian Economic History*, pp. 383-389.

22. Tony Wilden, *The Imaginary Canadian*, Vancouver: The Pulp Press, 1980.

23. See particularly, "The Teaching of Economic History in Canada", *Essays in Canadian Economic History*, 3-16; and "Adult Education and the University", in *The Bias of Communication*, pp. 203-214.

24. H.A Innis, *Essays in Canadian Economic History*, p. 399.

25. *Ibid.*, p. 403.

26. H.A. Innis, *The Strategy of Culture*, p. 16.

27. H.A. Innis, *Essays in Canadian Economic History*, p. 385.

28. H.A. Innis, *The Bias in Communication*, p. 82.

29. *Ibid*.

30. For Antonio Gramsci, this tension was the ground of the "organic intellectual".

31 H.A. Innis, *A History of The Canadian Pacific Railway*, p. 290.

32. See particularly Innis' introductory essay in *Empire and Communications*, Toronto: University of Toronto Press, 1972, pp. 3-11.

33. H.A. Innis, *Essays in Canadian Economic History*, p. 50.

34. Innis' most eloquent account of the oral culture of the Greeks is contained in his essay, "A Plea for Time", *The Bias of Communication*, p. 68; and in "The Oral Tradition and the Greeks", *Empire and Communications*, pp. 51-87.

35. H.A. Innis, *Empire and Communications*, p. 7.

36. Margaret Atwood, *Survival*, Toronto: Anansi, 1972, p. 32.

37. H.A. Innis, *The Fur Trade in Canada*, p. 386.

38. *Ibid*.

39. H.A. Innis, "The Penetrative Powers of the Price System", in *Essays in Canadian Economic History*, pp. 259-272.

40. H.A. Innis, *The Fur Trade in Canada*, pp. 6-19.

41. H.A. Innis, *A History of the Canadian Pacific Railway*, p. 294.

42. H.A. Innis, *The Cod Fisheries*, Toronto: University of Toronto Press, 1942, pp. 82-83.

43. H.A. Innis, *The Bias of Communication*, p. 64.

44. The study of such major "cultural disturbances" was the locus of Innis' cultural anthropology in *Empire and Communications*.

45. H.A. Innis, *The Bias of Communication*, pp. 87-89.

46. *Ibid*., p. 191.

47. See especially, *Empire and Communications*.

48. Innis' reflections on the "bias of communication" are developed at length in *Empire and Communications* and thematically presented in his classic essay, "The Bias of Communication", in *The Bias of Communication*, pp. 33-60.

49. Innis' image of the "stable society" as a desideratum contrasts sharply with McLuhan's vision of the mythic and integral society of "cosmic man".

50. See particularly William James' account of pluralism in his book, *Essays in Radical Empiricism: A Pluralistic Universe*, New York: Longmans, Green, 1943.

51. H.A. Innis, *The Bias of Communication*, p. 191.

52. *Ibid.*, p. 86.

53. An excellent account of L. Zea's critical sociology is provided in M. Weinstein's *The Polarity of Mexican Thought: Instrumentalism and Finalism*, University Park: the Pennsylvania State University Press, 1976, pp. 59-70.

54. This tension was at the heart of Mills' political thought.

55. Innis always privileged the biological model as a way of classifying, and then evaluating, the adaptive strategies deployed in the colonisation of the New World. Innis was attracted, in particular, to Thorstein Veblen's merger of biology and economy. See Innis' *Essays in Canadian Economic History*, pp. 17-26.

56. *Ibid.*, p. 24.

57. Innis approached each of the "staples commodities" through the discursive framework of biology. This is explicitly stated in his methodological comments on *The Fur Trade in Canada* and in *A History of the Canadian Pacific Railway*.

58. See particularly, "The Canadian Economy and the Depression", *Essays in Canadian Economic History*, pp. 123-140.

59. H.A. Innis, *Essays in Canadian Economic History*, p. 26.

60. See particularly, H.A. Innis, *The Fur Trade in Canada*, pp. 386-397 and *Empire and Communications*, pp. 3-11.

61. Graham Wallas, *Human Nature in Politics*, London: Constable & Company Ltd., 1948, p. 188.

62. What M. McLuhan identified as Innis' adoption of the social ecology of Robert Parks was actually one aspect only of a broader naturalistic discourse on the processed world of the staples economy.

63. H.A. Innis, *Empire and Communications*, pp. 75-80.

64. *Ibid.*, p. 9.

65. *Ibid.*, p. 7.

66. H.A. Innis, *The Bias of Communication*, pp. 49-50.

67. H.A. Innis, *Empire and Communications*, p. vii.

68. *Ibid.*, p. 9.

69. *Ibid.*, p. 54.

70. *Ibid.*, pp. 162-163.

71. Both McLuhan (*The Medium is the Massage*) and Innis ("A Plea for Time") appeal for a recovery of the mythic and integral experience of time.

72. H.A. Innis, *Empire and Communications*, p. 56.

73. "Drainage basins bring about centralisation; and submerged drainage basins decentralisation . . . Again, staple products coming down the St. Lawrence system made for a centralisation of products, whereas fishing from the numerous ports of an extended costs line made for decentralisation" H.A. Innis, *The Cod Fisheries*, p. 484.

74. See, for example, the striking similarity between Innis' description of the significance of the Nile (*Empire and Communications*, p. 12) and the St. Lawrence (*The Fur Trade in Canada*).

75. H.A. Innis, *Essays in Canadian Economic History*, p. 259.

76. H.A. Innis, *Empire and Communications*, p. 7.

77. *Ibid.*, pp. 5-11. For Innis, the staple is a medium of communication with its own semiurgical rules.

78. H.A. Innis, *The Strategy of Culture*, pp. 18-20.

79. Daniel Drache, "The Crisis of Canadian Political Economy", *Canadian Journal of Political and Social Theory*, Vol. 7, no. 3, (1983).

80. Raymond Morrow, "Deux pays pour vivre: Critical Sociology and the New Canadian Political Economy", *Canadian Journal of Political and Social Theory*, Vol. 6, no. 1-2, (1982), p. 198.

81. H.A. Innis, *Essays in Canadian Economic History*, p. 411.

82. Innis' classic account of American empire is provided in his essay, "The Military Implications of the American Constitution", *The Strategy of Culture*, pp. 21-45.

83. H.A. Innis, "Recent Developments in the Canadian Economy", in *Essays in Canadian Economic History*, p. 306.

84. H.A. Innis, *The Strategy of Culture*, p. 19.

85. H.A. Innis, "Political Implications of Unused Capacity", in *Essays in Canadian Economic History*, p. 382.

86. Karl Marx, "The Fetishism of the Commodity and the Secret Thereof", *Capital: A Critique of Political Economy*, Vol. 1, Moscow: Progress Publishers, 1954, pp. 76-87.

87. H.A. Innis, "The Penetrative Powers of the Price System" in *Essays in Canadian Economic History*, p. 260.

88. *Ibid.*, p. 271.

89. *Ibid.*, p. 263.

90. *Ibid.*, pp. 262-264.

91. In Innis' discourse, there was no discontinuity between the cultural productions (television, magazines, radio) of commercial empire and the more traditional industrial products.

92. Tom Naylor, "Canada in the European Age", *Canadian Journal of Political and Social Theory*, Vol. 7, no. 3, (1983), pp. 128-149.

93. See especially, H.A. Innis, *The Bias of Communication*, pp. 92-93.

94. It was, of course, Innis' thesis that sudden extensions of communication occasioned great cultural disturbances.

95. H.A. Innis, *The Bias of Communication*, p. 140.

96. *Ibid.*, p. 139.

97. *Ibid.*, p. 187.

98. *Ibid.*, p. 190.

99. This is, indeed, the central theme of Innis' *The Strategy of Culture*.

100. The concept of "missionary consciousness" as a description of the will to empire was developed by the American political philosopher Michael A. Weinstein.

101. H.A. Innis, *The Strategy of Culture*, p. 20.

102. *Ibid.*, p. 15.

103. *Ibid.*, p. 44.

104. This theme is developed forcefully in Innis' essay, "Recent Developments in the Canadian Economy", *Essays in Canadian Economic History*, pp. 291-308.

105. H.A. Innis, *Essays in Canadian Economic History*, p. 306.

---

5   1. See Don Theall, "McLuhan, the Toronto School of Communications and the Telematic Society", in *Technology, Culture and Power: A Canadian Discourse, CJPST/New World Perspectives*, forthcoming, Fall, 1985.

2. Michael Dorland, "Film and Memory: The Cinematic Style of Jean-Claude Labrecque", *Cinéma Canada*, No. 103, Jan., 1984, pp. 7-10.